The Myth of the Other

Lacan, Deleuze, Foucault, Bataille

Franco Rella

English Translation

Nelson Moe

PostModernPositions, Volume 7

Maisonneuve Press
Washington, D.C. 1994

Franco Rella, *The Myth of the Other: Lacan, Deleuze, Foucault, Bataille*

English translation by Nelson Moe

© copyright 1994 Maisonneuve Press
P.O. Box 2980 Washington, DC 20013-2980 USA
Originally published as *Il mito dell'altro: Lacan, Deleuze, Foucault* copyright 1978 by Giangiacomo Feltrinelli Editore, Milano, Italy.

All rights reserved. Brief quotations used in articles and reviews are encouraged provided clear acknowledgment to this book is given. For any other reproduction, please contact the publisher.

Maisonneuve Press is a division of the Institute for Advanced Cultural Studies, a non-profit organization devoted to social change through cultural analysis.

Printed in the US by BookCrafters, Fredricksburg, VA

Library of Congress Cataloging-in-Publication Data

Rella, Franco. 1944-
   [Il Mito dell'altro. English]
   The myth of the other : Lacan, Deleuze, Foucault, Bataille / Franco Rella; English translation, Nelson Moe.
      p. cm. -- (PostModernPostitions ; vol. 7)
   Includes bibliographical references and index.
   ISBN 0-944624-20-0 cl. / ISBN 0-944624-21-9 pa.
     1. Philosophy--France--History--20th Century.
2. Postmodernism--History. 3. Lacan, Jacques, 1901- .
4. Deleuze, Gilles. 5. Foucault, Michel. 6. Bataille, Georges, 1897-1962. I. Title. II. Series.
B2421.R43 1994   93-23435
194-dc20   CIP

6º
underlining

The Myth of the Other

PostModernPositions
volume seven

Contents

Translator's Preface	1
Author's Preface to the North American Edition	5

Part One

Preface	13
Introduction	14
The Myth of the Other	27
The Foucault Apparatus	57

Part Two

Beauty's Ulterior Gaze	81
I. An Erratic Movement	81
II. The Engima	86
III. The Light of Evil	90
IV. The Double Economy	94
V. Desire and Transfiguration	97
VI. The Look of Beauty	100
Notes and References	107
Index	123

The Myth of the Other

Translator's Preface

Until quite recently, Italy has represented a substantial *terra incognita* on the North American map of contemporary critical and philosophical inquiry, a landscape which, if depicted in the guise of the famous *New Yorker* cover, would appear in the distance across the sea as a mountain marked "Umberto Eco" and perhaps, to those with keener eyes, as a mound marked "Gianni Vattimo." Over the past few years, however, this unknown territory has gradually begun to be filled in by the publication of a number of philosophical and critical texts by Italians in English translation. It is within the context of this attempt to make the voices of Italy a part of our contemporary critical conversation that I have chosen to "bring over" *The Myth of the Other: Lacan, Deleuze, Foucault, Bataille* by Franco Rella, a brief work by one of Italy's most extraordinary younger philosophers.

From the title of the book, it is immediately apparent that the subject under consideration is not, in fact, a particularly Italian one but rather concerns four of the most influential French theorists on the contemporary critical scene. What is Italian about the book instead is the critical perspective it brings to bear on these authors, the specific questions it asks of them. My choice to translate *The Myth of the Other* was, in other words, prompted by the desire to offer North American readers of French theory another perspective on this material, one which simultaneously works out of a proximity to the continental philosophical terrain on which these theories have arisen and out of its own Italian distance from it.

The theoretical network in which this translation is situated can therefore be seen as a triangle. From the point occupied by the French theorists under consideration, two sides extend to the North American and Italian critical communities that have devoted their attention to them. The third side which would then connect these two points is the English translation of *The Myth of the Other*. The translation aims in other words to present Rella reading Lacan-Deleuze-Foucault-Bataille to North American readers of these same authors. The movements through this triangular circuit are of course not synchronous but staggered in time, with the main part of Rella's response dating back to 1977, the product—as Rella notes in his preface to this edition—of a specific moment in Italian intellectual and political history.

It may be helpful here to consider a few aspects of Rella's work which are not self-evident in the pages that follow, a few of the intellectual and political contexts specific to Italy which have had a significant impact upon his philosophical production.

Firstly, like the majority of Italian thinkers on the Left, Rella writes within a horizon of concerns powerfully structured by Marxist thought, by the traditional strength of Marxism in the institutions of Italian society and culture. In such an intellectual environment, it is not a question of being or not being "a Marxist" in some discrete, card-carrying sense, but rather of participating in a community of shared concerns which have been largely shaped by the Marxist tradition.[1] As the reader of the following pages will note, *The Myth of the Other* is by no means a Marxist text. And yet the original publication of the book in a series titled "Opuscoli Marxisti" (Brief Marxist Works) attests precisely to its location within the Marxist "cultural dominant" present in Italy during the 1960s and 1970s.[2]

At the same time, these decades in Italy were characterized by a climate of intense political contestation, which erupted most dramatically in the movements of 1968 and the terrorism of the mid-1970s. Rella came of age as a philosopher in the midst of these pressures, which invested both the academy and the Left as a whole. *The Myth of the Other* is then, among other things, a document of his engagement with the set of philosophical problems which arose on the terrain of this social and political upheaval.

A second key feature of Rella's work is his persistent exploration of what he calls the "region which lies on the border between literature and philosophy." In the preface to one of his most powerful books, *Il silenzio e le parole* (1981) Rella writes: "The choice of this space is based upon my conviction that here, in the transit and relationship between two forms of thought, some of the most radical models of critical analysis of the real in this century have been produced, models which evince a decisive change in the conceptual frameworks and images of thought that have been heretofore dominant." For Rella, this space consists specifically of the set of turn-of-the-century German and Austrian thinkers to whom he has devoted close attention throughout his career—above all Nietzsche, Freud, Rilke, Kafka, Benjamin, and Musil, traces of whom can all be found in *The Myth of the Other*. To a very great extent, Rella's work is a product of his engagement with these thinkers, an engagement by no means atypical for Italian philosophers and critics of his generation.

Finally, Rella's work needs to be situated in the context of contemporary Italian philosophy.[3] To a considerable extent his work is the fruit of collaboration and dialogue with thinkers like Remo Bodei, Aldo Gargani, Massimo Cacciari, Pier Aldo Rovatti and Salvatore Veca, who, in the years during which *The Myth of the Other* was written, were all engaged in a more or less explicit interrogation of what was known as "the crisis of reason," a crisis which, while intimately related to the political crisis of the time, more generally concerned the exhaustion of that "classical rationality [which] has presented itself for hundreds of years with the cachets and claims to authority of a natural, necessary and a priori structure."[4] As the reader will see, for Rella the productive tensions of this crisis need to be explored, not resolved or evaded through the construction of a "myth of the other."

These then are a few of the Italian coordinates along which Rella's philosophical activity, and *The Myth of the Other* in particular, can be situated. They of course represent only one, local, dimension of his work, the one probably least familiar to North-American readers. The rest lies beyond the scope of this preface, in the reader's own engagement with Rella in the pages that follow.

Wherever possible, reference has been made to accessible English editions of texts which first appeared in other languages, but I have occasionally revised the translations or provided my own.

I wish to thank Karen Van Dyck for her comments on the translation, Robert Merrill of Maisonneuve Press for his crucial interest in and support for the project, and Franco Rella for his generous collaboration throughout.

Nelson Moe

Author's Preface

to the North American Edition

The Myth of the Other was written in the second half of the 1970s within a political horizon—specifically, that of Italy—characterized by a widespread conflictuality which seemed in many ways to have repudiated reason and thus presented itself as an absolute negation incapable of *ethically* positing itself within the context of existing social antagonisms. This "essay," to give a precise historical referent, was written during the months of the imprisonment and assassination of Aldo Moro by the Red Brigade terrorist group.

Even non-academic philosophical reflection on the contradictions of late (or post-) modernity seemed unable to move beyond this negative horizon. Great thinkers like Lacan or Foucault were immediately assimilated as cartographers of reason's dissolution instead of as the proponents of a new possible reading of the great tensions that characterize our epoch.

Intellectuals who sought to react to this sort of "pulverization" of reason (and I am thinking, for example, of Massimo Cacciari, Remo Bodei, Aldo Gargani) put forth the hypothesis that one should not speak of reason's decline but rather of its crisis. And the concept of "crisis," often deriving primarily from a reconsideration of

Viennese thought of the first decades of this century, appeared capable of explaining the singularity, the groups and subjects that could not be contained within a unitary political, ethical and theoretical framework. In those same years Gianni Vattimo offered his version of the "crisis of reason." He was initiating, that is, his reflection on this crisis as the modality in which Being presents itself ("happens") to existence in our epoch. It is starting from here that in successive years Vattimo would come to theorize a "weak" subject and thought which should not "resist" this decline but rather decline with Being.

The Myth of the Other inserted itself within this perspective. It too moved within the space of the "crisis of reason," but sought to find within it the forms of a new capacity to establish relations with the real—and, in this case, with a *politically determinate real*.

In my later books, from *Il Silenzio e le parole* (1981) to *Bellezza e verita* (1990), I have sought to trace the profile of a "not-solely-reasoning reason," which was capable of moving also through images and contexts traditionally considered impracticable by philosophy. The subject bearing this "reason" is the subject of our epoch: the subject of the *limen*, of the border, understood not as exclusion but as the potential for transit between subject and subject, between subjects and things. A subject, in a word, capable of relating to alterity without mythologizing it. The border, or the threshold, thus became the very site of difference: that *regio dissimilitudinis* which from the beginning—from Plato—*all* of Western thought has opposed.

The concept of *threshold* is that which illuminates all of Benjamin's *Passagen-Werk*, perhaps the most widely discussed thinker in Italy during the early 1980s. And nearly all "thinkers of the crisis" (save Vattimo, who has coherently developed his "weak," tendentially infinite hermeneutic) have gone beyond the concept of crisis, towards new "thresholds" of reason: from Massimo Cacciari's attempt to articulate philosophy and theology together, to Bodei's rediscovery of Hölderlinian tragedy, or Sergio Givone's rediscovery of Dostoyevskian tragedy.

These have been important reflections, that have lead me to find in this threshold a new ethical and political horizon: political struggle understood, then, as a struggle for difference.

Truth without justice, as the Greek tragedians knew, is nothing. Dostoyevsky knew it as well when, in *The Idiot*, he wrote, "that which you have written is only truth, therefore it is *unjust*." The truth is unjust because it excludes from itself not only the other, the un-truth, but also their difference. What is then the threshold, or liminal concept, that must hold together the truth and its opposite, so that there is not *adikia*, injustice?

Dostoyevsky had a name for this "threshold." He called it beauty, and in *The Idiot* he writes that "beauty will save the world" because, as he writes in *The Brothers Karamazov* as well, beauty contains all contradictions and all ways. It is a recovery, beyond philosophy, of the great tragic thought which Hölderin first put back into play within the field of modernity, he too affirming that without the recognition of difference within unity, without the recognition of a unity made of contradictory elements, there is no *beauty* and therefore no thought.

Starting out from this point of view it is possible to discover a hidden tradition within modernity, from Hölderin to Simone Weil, that speaks of contradiction calling it by the name of beauty, a tradition that has no aesthetic prominence in the strict sense, but which poses ethical and political objectives for itself. It posits itself in fact as a thought that wishes to be worthy of the extreme conditions of our time.

These are the theoretical coordinates in which my research moves at the present time: around the *form* capable of expressing difference, of *preserving it*. Around the "name" of a "beauty" that, as Simone Weil writes, would be obscene to reduce to the dimension of aesthetic appreciation, or even that of art theory.

And yet the fundamental inspiration is still that of *The Myth of the Other*: the concern, precisely, that the immense richness of the diverse not be lost in a mythology of alterity, which simply opposes to reason a form of non-reason; or, in the best of cases, which sets up in opposition to classical reason, a critical reason, a reason of the crisis, transforming itself into a critique of ideology which has been the limit against which the most acute Italian philosophical reflection of the 1970s has come up and, in part, exhausted itself.

It is this context that I have tried to take into account for this new edition of the *Myth of the Other*, twelve years after its first publication.

In these twelve years it is not only my theoretical perspective that has changed: the immediate referents of *The Myth of the Other* have changed as well. Lacan is dead, leaving an immense inheritance which must be evaluated today in light of the collapse of that Lacanianism which wrapped his thought in a thick rhetorical curtain, quasi-sacral and hermetic. Foucault is dead too, but leaving in the "Introduction" to his last writings the sense of a new tension: the attempt to reconstruct a genesis of subjectivity which returns to the center of his theoretical concerns after a long peroration on the death of the subject. Deleuze seems to have abandoned his rhizomatic vision of the world, taking refuge in a more systematic perspective. Lyotard, beginning with a rereading of Kant, seems engaged today in a reconstruction of phenomenology within the framework of a legitimation of contemporary signifying practices.

Given this historical change, and my own personal change, it has seemed impossible to me to proceed by way of a pure and simple up-dating of *The Myth of the Other*. I have preferred to leave it unaltered *with its own reasons*, but adding to it a second part: a kind of *Myth of the Other II*. In this second part, I analyze the work of Georges Bataille, who is perhaps at the base of mythologies of alterity considered in my work from 1978, but within the mirror of the thought of Simone Weil, who leads us to that concept of beauty which is not aesthetic, but theoretical, ethical and political that is at the center of my present research. In fact, the essay "Beauty's Ulterior Gaze" that constitutes Part II of *The Myth of the Other* in this new format is, so to speak, the first move of my future work on eros and logos, a move toward a theory and ethics of beauty [published in 1991 as *L'enigma della bellezza*—Trans.].

I thank Bollati Boringhieri Publishers who have permitted me to reproduce the essay "Beauty's Ulterior Gaze," which was written as an introduction to the Italian edition of Bataille's *La part maudite*, in this new context.

I thank Nelson Moe, the translator of the English edition of *The Myth of the Other*, with whom I discussed the problems and structure of the book.

This adventure of thought has been made possible by an intense rapport with my wife, Sandra Dorigotti, to whom I dedicate this book in its new form.

Franco Rella

Part One . . .

The Myth of the Other

The Foucault Apparatus

Preface

This essay is part of a more extended work which, beginning with certain manifestations of Freudian critique, proposes to investigate certain models and forms of the rationality which is emerging within our historical space. Here the most "plural" and disseminative strategies are taken into consideration, which occupy a highly significant area of this space and which have assumed a notable political import in recent years.

The reading of these strategies which this essay offers is an openly partial one. I have not been interested in explaining them, but rather in articulating them as critical and problematic signs of a more widespread process which has, in my view, been unfolding. I am therefore quite aware that these positions may appear to have a solidity which they do not in fact possess. At the same time, it is natural that a given analytic work leave margins of conflictual resistance, on the basis of which the analysis itself can be put into question. This is a task that I myself in fact propose.

I have utilized for this essay a number of materials which I had already elaborated in the past, reworking them amply. The most direct reference is "Nel nome di Freud. Il mito dell'altro," in *Aut Aut* 161 (1977), and "Introduzione," in *Il dispositivo Foucault* (Venezia: Cluva, 1977).

Introduction

> . . . O madness of discourse,
> That cause sets up with and against itself,
> Bi-fold authority, where reason can revolt
> Without perdition, and loss assume all reason
> Without revolt. . . .
> —*Troilus and Cressida*, V.ii.

The crisis of the classical system, the crisis within which we move today, has historically signified the end of the illusion that the multiplicity of languages could be reconstituted within a single comprehensive language capable of holding sway over the contradictory plurality of the real. But what has suffered a crisis in not only a unitary model of reason, however flexible and attentive to the negative, the different and the contradictory as the Hegelian model in fact is.[5] What has suffered a crisis is also its mechanisms, its discourses, its criteria of control and verification. A whole constellation of rationalities and discourses have arisen in opposition to this model of classical reason which are the products of diverse emergent social groups and classes, the products of the expansion of the "sphere of conscious protagonists of social existence." "One has the historical perception of something in excess," writes Remo Bodei, "of something that cannot be contained within the rules as they have been passed down, just as it cannot be contained within a single mode of reason and a single discourse."[6]

But to take stock of this crisis, to work and act within it, does not mean to repudiate "rationality and control," does not mean "to succumb to the schizophrenia of rationalities which are in principle incommunicable."[7] The crisis consists not only of disorder and ill: it is an imbalance but also a tension towards new orders. The contradictions cannot be "resolved," but rather transformed. The terrain for this transformation is undoubtedly political; it is the struggle, the fight "for the *proliferation of modes of reason* and separate protocols, for the conquest of zones, of regions of thought with different tempos, disjunctions, movements, dispersions. Yet, at the same time, it is a fight to *remove the obstacles* which are set up within the channels of communication between knowledges and which stand in turn between these knowledges and the 'common' consciousness or consciousnesses which are not directly involved in the field of research, so as to involve the wider masses, freeing the subordinate and so-called minor knowledges and techniques from their subjection to 'Science' and 'Technology.'"[8]

This "liberation" takes place through a struggle, this process of communication through a clash. I believe, in fact, that the reciprocal *untranslatability* of discourses and modes of reason and knowledge which constitute the critical constellation within which we move does not at all mean *autonomy*. These separate, untranslatable discourses impinge upon one another to such an extent that they constantly put into question their very constitution, their very existence as techniques and instruments for representing and dominating the real. "Autonomy" understood as the "self-sufficiency" of a discourse (the political, for example),[9] or the emphasis upon difference, upon the rhizomatic dispersion of every discourse, every gesture, desire, need inevitably ends up positioning itself within a desire for a lost totality, as the specular reverse of a totalizing and unitary mode of reason.

"To change the rules of the game," to construct new orders, means that "it is not sufficient to govern (better) things as they exist" and, at the same time, that "it is necessary to have the courage to 'represent' as well that which is *destructive*."[10] This *political labor* cannot take place under the protection of a discourse or technique which is guaranteed in relation to other emergent discourses that exert pressure upon it, which clash against it. Nor can it take place under the illusion of being outside every discourse within the pure flux of desire, within its uncontainable and rhizomatic proliferation. "To represent" as well "that which is destructive" means to represent as well the destruction, the smashing of a given discourse's privilege—even as we grant its separateness and partiality, to destroy the metaphysics of alterity and difference.

2. To sketch, even summarily, the map of this constellation, of the space of *this crisis*, is a task that cannot be deferred or eluded from the moment that the pressure of the "desperate destroyers"[11] towards forms of regressive irrationalism appears to be strongest. Deleuze's desire without an object, Lyotard's libidinal economy, the dispersion of power in Foucault and the Lacanianism of the Left that we will be considering in the following pages are nothing but a particular "region" within the larger constellation of the neo-classical (or post-classical) reason of plurality and contradiction. Within this "constellation" and this "critical" space we find as well the theory of needs, the revision of Marxism (or of one of its traditions) that assesses the "scientific program of Marx" with its "hidden metaphysics," that sees the "recognition of the neo-classical heritage"[12] as an antidote to the metaphysics of progress, of transparency, of the translatability of discourses into a strong, monolithic discourse.[13]

But why, within this constellation, concern ourselves with this particular region, which is apparently its extreme margin? For two principal reasons, it seems to me. First, because it is more important today to settle accounts with what is passing directly through our space than to linger to confute late-dialectic mythologies. Secondly, because it is precisely within this extreme margin of *our* space that we can read the temptation to transform the negative of classical reason into a direct positivity, to repropose its dis-values as values: the temptation to position ourselves beyond the crisis and its *productive* conditions.

We must rebel against the statutes of a reason that has expelled from itself practices, behaviors, determinate needs, without losing ourselves, without losing reason itself, in order to reconstruct its conflictual reality, *the reality of its conflicts*. Vice versa, the rhizomatic temptation is that of a disintegrated form of reason that tends to posit itself as whole, to call itself whole: untouched and untouchable in its absolute alterity. This, in my opinion, is an attempt to "escape" from the crisis by irrationalistic means: instead of calling into question one notion of rationality and power as a system of exclusions and prohibitions, it posits itself straightaway as an extreme attempt at recomposition. The totality of the body without organs of Deleuze and Guattari, the fullness of the libidinal economy of Lyotard, the Truth of the language of the Other that founds every "dialect" for the Lacanians constitute themselves again as "petrified words"[14] which Nietzsche invited us to break in order to *go beyond*, like those "hyperbolic expressions" which, Kafka wrote, "do not actually describe, but rather skirt the right description with incredible rapidity."[15]

In fact, if the disciplinary apparatuses through which in the past only that which kept the dominant regime of reason intact was admitted to the Parthenon of rationality are to be criticized; if, conversely, all that which signalled its crisis was rejected into the ghetto of irrationality, we certainly cannot content ourselves with a pure and simple reversal—by making a Parthenon of the ghetto and vice versa. The deconstruction of the values and rituals upon which the power of the dominant mode of reason was based (or, of the dominion that asserted its right to determine what is right) cannot limit itself to the simple "elevation" of its dis-values to the status of new values. It would once again entail the proposal of a mythology insofar as it would involve the assumption of practices and behaviors that are desperately and fiercely incapable of "working" the crisis, of crossing it and transforming it.

The presence of a formidable slogan on the political scene such as "the personal is political," which signals that "the very constitution of individuality and subjectivity has been modified"[16] in a radical fashion, cannot but have its effect upon political discourse and practice. There is no autonomy that can elude this confrontation and clash that break out within each discourse, a contradiction that pushes at its "limits," upon its statutes, upon its criteria of practical and theoretical legitimation—which pushes, in a word, to change the rules of the game. But this can only happen if this "phrase" is truly posited as a "node" within that process whereby a series of historically determinate needs *become political*, if it helps us to demonstrate and transform these needs: to *interpret* them.

But to read in this "phrase," instead, the *immediate, true* expression of a natural totality *beyond contradictions* means thinking, illusorily, that certain subjects exist which are immune (or redeemed) from contradiction, subjects which precisely because of their "purity" (or "impurity"—the insane, the marginal, etc.) are *other* from the society and the history in which we live, bearers of *needs* and *values* that are inevitably incomprehensible to any form of reason. In fact—so goes the "illusion"—*autonomy* is the process of self-valorization, autonomy is that "existence within the happiness of the proletariat's independent struggle" through which "the proletariat's assault on the heavens is organized."[17]

3. The idealization of the negative that is also within *our* space, the constellation that we have sketched out above, becomes the struggle for those margins "incomprehensible" to the dominant regime of reason to affirm themselves qua spaces of marginalization and exclusion. The ill that this society expels can only be our good, our value. Yet however much struggle and violence are organized around this "value," it ends up positing itself as the confirmation of that regime of exclusive reason and power; the desert of marginalization is the desert of a violence without a name or, better, of a violence that can only speak through the "names" offered it by the mythology of the dominant.

This, then, is not only one of the most extreme developments of "neo-classical," "plural" reason; it is also the "site" in which it seeks to reconvert itself into "truth," to refound itself on "true" values. Dispersion becomes a kind of "guarantee" of a complete word which lies elsewhere, of a natural subjectivity that is *other* from the society and the contradictions which traverse and produce it. In a field quite opposed to this constellation, yet curiously convergent with it, seems to me the appeal (precisely contra Marx and Freud) to the certainty of facts that one finds in the epistemology of Lakatos[18] or in Kuhn's attempt to establish a "normality" of science even within its revolutions.[19]

One of the most powerful countervailing forces with respect to this attempt to reconvert plurality into another normality, into a different totality, is undoubtedly constituted by the "name" of Freud. And it is not an accident that the debate on Freud opened up before, or at least with greater scope than, other assessments of "negative thought"—before the present-day engagement with Nietzsche, Weber, Wittgenstein or Heidegger—and that it has had and continues to have a stronger political impact.

It seems to me that Freud grasped more surely than any other theorist of the discourses of the twentieth-century crisis the plurality of dialects that exist within the space of subjectivity. But not only this. Freud also understood that the process of "rationalization" of separate and non-universal discourses is a *compromise formation* that tends to render itself unassailable to criticism, in the same way that the great ideological formations bent on remedying the "discontent of civilization" attempted to render themselves unassailable. The critical task therefore, also within these separate and rationalized languages in their very condition of separateness, is to construct their contradictory reality, and this is a truly *interminable* task. Only practice itself, Freud writes in "Analysis Terminable and Interminable," "decides" the (provisional) end of an analysis.[20]

But "interminable analysis" signifies in fact the awareness that certain elements erupt within these discourses, within the psychoanalytic discourse itself (which enjoys no special privilege), which are heterogeneous to it, elements which must find a "reason" for existing which does not eliminate their heterogeneity, simply displacing them.

This is the challenge, the confrontation, taking place today around the name of Freud. The temptation to repropose a full subjectivity (whether it be of an immediate or indeterminate need, or of the desire without object) clashes here with Freud's theoretical elaborations. And for this reason it is *symptomatic* that many of the rhizomatic operations, the most plural and dispersive ones, have acted and worked under the sign of Lacan.

Lacan undoubtedly represents the most significant and powerful of the attempts of "philosophical" rationality to bring Freud back to his "truth." When Lacan speaks of the true Freud, the accent falls precisely on this "truth," which, as Lacan writes, "asserts itself to the discredit of reason," opening the way "in the arid climate of scientism," so as to "recreate the human spirit." The truth is the "cause causing every effect," and it manifests itself in the fictive structure of our discourse. Plurality does not exist but rather only a fallacy that lets the truth speak through its web.

The Other is precisely the "witness" to the truth, of which the analyst, with his discourse and his silence, is lord and master.[21] Freud recognized in the formations of ideology and signification a kernal of historical truth that extends to the shell that contains it in the form of a "conviction of truth" so as to render the shell safe from criticism. The analysis of this "conviction" is a labor of radical historicization of the "truth" that it contains. Lacan proposes instead a truth that articulates itself without qualifications, that is the cause and foundation of every discourse, that situates itself beyond history (the site of its pure manifestation) and civilization ("*cloaca maxima*").[22]

Why, then, does the most plural and rhizomatic expression of neo-classical reason meet up with a project of philosophical unification of the subject and reality which, in its most recent manifestations, assumes an actual theological tendency?[23] Why this necessity to re-traverse the great Lacanian recomposition?

This is the sign that the exacerbation of neo-classical discourse in its elaborations by Deleuze and Guattari, but also by Foucault, becomes the formidable reversal of a formidably unitary reason; the most extremely rhizomatic model, even if it articulates itself in the negative, is consonant with the unitary model of philosophical reason as it manifests itself, for example, in Lacan. The no-place of Lacan's Other and the "elsewhere" of Deleuze and Guattari end up being the same place: the utopian "good-place" beyond the contradictions that constitute our historical space.

4. The attraction of a "strong" mode of reason is present, however, in other regions of this constellation as well. Alongside, or right in front of, the emphasis upon difference there are various other attempts to found a language which, while calling itself separate and non-universal, posits itself however as a normative grammar by way of a series of prohibitions and exclusions. We thus once more see the realization of a model of reason which,

having rid itself of non-universality, reconstitutes itself as a "strong" reason within a "strong" language which ends up yet again dictating unanalyzed laws, behaviors, practices.

I have already noted that a part of contemporary epistemological discourse functions in this way, that is, that it "celebrates with the expenditure of great intellectual energy a ritual motivated by the need to protect an order of intellectual practice from alternative, non-conventional models of rationality exhibited be emergent social groups and classes."[24] These are actual defensive rituals which arise out of the need to negate the representation of that which appears "destructive," that is, the "innovative and unsettling character of the crisis,"[25] and which powerfully reveal the desire to reconstitute the plurality of the real and of cognitive practices in a norm of legitimation that presents itself as an extra-cognitive "value" as such.

But this temptation seems to me strong in the discourse of the autonomy of the political as well, as least there where it presents itself as "the only true rationality possible within the modern state."[26] In this context, every element within the crisis of the objective mechanisms of the state must, if it is to count, be mediated by, translated into this language, which thus assumes a privileged weight and which excludes, *does not represent* the other: emergent social groups, subjects, the realities that do not speak this language or, better, that are not "comprehended" by the rules of this language. Certainly Asor Rosa is right: to write poetry "is not and can never be the same thing as doing politics."[27] But is it possible to change the rules of the game, even of *this* game, without *seeing* all the cards? Or playing on only one table? Or don't we have to recognize that the plurality of the real is not pure and simple pluralism? It is thus not a question of recognizing the legitimacy ("legality") of poetry alongside politics (and alongside all the other languages as well) but of recognizing how these affect one another, clash with one another, how the contradictions produced out of this contradiction traverse them, move within their body. Isn't this what Wittgenstein meant when he denounced his own "preconceived idea of crystalline purity"? When he affirmed the necessity of "ploughing up the whole of language" there where a "mythology is deposited"?[28]

The contradictory plurality of the real is by no means "tamed" when we have divided it up and distributed the great classical dominion into a series of minor, specific, peripheral ones, separate from one another. For having taken stock of the impossibility of a general dominion of the real, as well as of a general theory that unifies all languages in a single one—be it of politics or of the unconscious—we have not thereby authorized a norm of exclusion that grants us certainty within our dominion, within our language, within our techniques.

The analysis is interminable. It is not, as Cacciari notes, a "Critique in general" but "an effective process of crisis, laid bare in its determinate contradictions."[29] This *rational* project of laying bare the contradictions so as to manage them is one that we cannot relinquish.

The complexity of the rational enterprise "incorporates within its perspective," in the words of Salvatore Veca, "a risk. Freed from ontological 'foundations,' it can obtain objectivity within the domain of the results it obtains; but it can also fail or lose the objectivity that has been acquired, be forced to give it up. In any case, we could say, objectivity is a possible but not necessary result, never a presupposition." On the contrary, it is necessary to perform a "disintegrative" strategy with respect to every objectivity that posits itself as a presupposition: the *limits* of the presupposed objectivity must be forced beginning precisely with those "heterogeneous materials that resist and reveal a persistent irreducibility."[30]

The choice of a plural mode of reason is not a "vocation" but arises from the need to make sense of that which in the unitary mode of reason remains incomprehensible.

Ours is then a *rational* project, without the least temptation to elevate plurality to a metaphysics of difference, to a desperate and bedazzled dissemination that has turned its back on the task of knowing and transforming reality and which therefore limits itself to a sort of enchantment of the abyss, or an assiduous cataloguing and archaeology of desperate events. "We want, in short," as Remo Bodei writes, "in Hölderlinian language, to keep rationality vigilant at the edge of the 'aorgic,' the multiple, the new to-be-received."[31] In fact, if we have renounced the great "comprehensive, exhaustive and definitive" theories for "the laborious, paltry and fragmentary attempts at explanation which are the most we are able to achieve," similarly we know that "science is not an illusion," that "it would be [an illusion] to suppose that what science cannot give us we can get from elsewhere."[32] And no confirmation of this fact can occur outside of the space of knowledge and struggle, outside of an "extremely difficult and risky engagement with language, with positions, with tradition"[33]—an engagement with *our* own language, *our* own position, *our* own tradition.

The rhizomatic area that I will attempt to explore in these pages is that in which this task is avoided most. It is also that in which the temptation is strongest to reconstitute a space where the incommunicability between different languages becomes the site of a truth beyond all knowledge and communication. We do not speak but, rather, are spoken by the Other and its truth. This other cannot be known because every act of knowing is an act of strangulation (Deleuze) or because every interpretation is the imposition of a relation of forces (Foucault). And yet it is necessary to move beyond this state of impotency: "Ignorance," writes Freud, "is ignorance; no right to believe anything can be derived from it."[34]

It is necessary to break through this barrier as well, behind which the truth establishes itself and hides in incommunicability. It is the "real genius" that Benjamin saw in Kafka: "he sacrificed truth for the sake of clinging to transmissibility." But outside of this choice there are nothing but the products of dissolution: on the one hand "the rumor about the true things," on the other, folly.[35] The "rumor about the true things" can protect us from folly, from contradictions, from reality, but it does not bring us one step closer to knowing it, to representing and controlling it: towards the *ability to control it*. And this, at bottom, is the key question.

The Myth of the Other

> My conscience hath a thousand several tongues,
> and every tongue brings in a several tale. . . .
> —*Richard III*, V.iii

In recent years we have been witness to a thorough-going "idealization of the negative,"[36] even on the part of groups situating themselves in radically anti-capitalist positions and who express not only a profound discontent but also a great positive charge, new needs and new forms of rationality which call into question the orders established by the dominant regime of reason, by its discourses and techniques. But alongside this "positive" aspect we are witnessing as well the establishment of the illusion that one can arrive, possibly through a *single* revolutionary break, in a linear and direct fashion, at something *other* than the existing state of things. It is at this level that we are witnessing a "general deterioration of the political dimension"[37] and an emphasis on needs and on the individual dimension which, insofar as they are *immediately* antagonistic to established society, assume the form of a real and true "idealization." It is, as Giovanni Jervis writes, "the desire to be immediately outside of the rules and the norms of capital, to leap over all the mediations and even the constructive dimension of political action itself: and this means . . . to want to have the radical break without the *praxis*. But this leads to an idealistic illusion. On the one hand the construction, the project, is substituted by an itinerary of entirely ideal reversal, often of a tendentially religious type. On the other, one exults in the immediacy of the act viewed as *subversive*, as an end in itself—in reality in the presumptuous violence of subjectivism."[38]

The plurality of contradictions that move through the social body and determine it is thus reduced to a dialectic of "norm" and "deviation," one which ends up "passively accepting the definitions of deviation set down by the dominant ideology, only rehabilitating *ipso facto* every form of deviation as subversive (according to a pseudo-syllogism: 'that which is revolutionary is persecuted and repressed; *therefore* that which is persecuted and repressed is revolutionary')."[39] The "flight from politics" thus assumes the connotations of an "auto-valorization" of the self as alterity, outside of and incomprehensible to the discourse of politics or to any discourse that isn't the direct expression of one's own immediate, individual desires which are presented as "other," "new," "different," and for that reason laden with value—values which are presented in fact as "new values."

The simplification of the complexity of the historical and political space that we occupy into terms of "norm" and "deviation" (or "dissidence")[40] ends up bestowing an ideological unity on a reality which is in fact plural, divided and contradictory: it becomes itself the desire for this reconstitution. And it is this "simplification" and this "desire" that have determined the success of a discourse such as that of the "psychoanalysm of the Left" which has no doubt offered a response, however confused and contradictory, to the need to re-evaluate the space of the subjective, of the "private" and "personal," but which has also translated itself into an illusory and triumphalistic exaltation of the omnipotence of the unconscious (if not of the psychoanalyst).

The unconscious, desire, the Other *speaks*. The psychoanalyst, master of this speech, can teach us to listen to it, insofar as it only manifests itself in the error, the sin, the fallacy of "normal" language—of the language of the "norm," of power and the law. And the "fallacy" of this "normal" language is illness, deviation, the "norm's" other face: madness and schizophrenia.

I believe that this space, precisely because it is the space of the crisis that we find ourselves in, must be traversed. To reject it as a pure and simple "anomaly" would not only confirm it as such, but would cover up something that is rooted deeply in our languages, even if with other forms and other "names": the desire for certainty, for a foundation, for value, even in opposition to the reality principle, the reality in which we are immersed and work.

2. The "idealization of the negative," of the Other, which "speaks" the language of the psychoanalyst, passes through the attempt to liquidate the immense demystificatory potential of Freudian analysis. The unconscious in Freud does not speak the language of the Other but speaks "many dialects," which cannot be composed or translated into a *single* language. Moreover, it does not speak directly: "We deduce its existence . . . from its effects."[41] The analyst does not therefore discover a hidden and mysterious reality, but *works* the various signifying formations— from the individual ones to the social and collective—precisely in order to "construct" the plurality of languages which the operations of defense—here too both individual and social—seek to reduce to a unity, to transparency, to the clarity of a uniform relationship with one reality posited as univocal.

There is no room in Freud for a natural truth. What he calls "material truth" is always off-stage. In analysis one always encounters a "historical truth" which the subject seeks to extend to the whole bundle that constitutes the signifying formation through which he enters into contact with the real and tries to control it. The "conviction" of truth will therefore protect this formation from the contradictions which move through it and continually call it into question. Analysis is therefore a labor of radical historicization which by deconstructing and *analyzing* that conviction of truth constructs the contradictions that it wished to "resolve" with this conviction. Delirium is also an attempt to heal, to cure and resolve contradictions through the conviction of truth. But what happens in delirium happens also in the great ideological formations.

"If we consider mankind as a whole and substitute it for the single human individual, we discover that it too has developed delusions which are inaccessible to logical criticism and which contradict reality. If, in spite of this, they are able to exert an extraordinary power over men, investigation leads us to the same explanation as in the case of the individual. They owe their power to the element of *historical truth* which they have brought up from the repression of the forgotten and primeval past."[42]

But analysis itself cannot enjoy any special privilege, cannot be translated into a "general critique," a kind of "totalizing coherency";[43] it can only constitute the space for the laying bare of determinate contradictions, of the bundle of relations which constitute its object. The analytic *construction*, in fact, never reaches a foundation where, as Freud himself writes in *On Narcissism*, "everything rests." The analysis is *unendliche*, interminable. Only the analytic practice itself can "decide" the provisional end of the analysis.[44]

The object of analysis is not therefore the celebration of the unconscious or the discovery of a truth seized from oblivion or the achievement of a full, intact subject. Freud's object, like Nietzsche's, is precisely the "power of truth," its power which is "extraordinary" and "inaccessible to criticism," even when its formations "contradict reality." Outside of this reality there exists no lost homeland, no possibility of escape from alienation—the Freudian *Unheimliche*[45]—from *this* plurality, from this network of contradictions that characterize and "perturb" our desire. "We cannot escape this world. We're always within it."[46] Here is the site of struggle: in this assiduous practice of construction and transformation of the power of "truth," in order to construct another power.

The "leftovers," the "refuse" of classical reason, the heterogeneous are not taken up as another truth but as the margin from which to begin to traverse and re-elaborate and transform the entire process of rationalization:[47] not, in the first place at least, to heal. Therapy is only one of the effects of the analytical activity, and not even the most important one at that.[48] Certainly the establishment of a different relationship with that which has been discarded and displaced can function too as a cure, but, as Freud writes: "After forty-one years of medical activity, my self-knowledge tells me that I have never really been a doctor in the proper sense. I became a doctor through being compelled to deviate from my original purpose; and the triumph of my life lies in my having, after a long and roundabout journey, found my way back to my earliest path. I have no knowledge of having had any craving in my early childhood to help suffering humanity."[49]

Thus as Freud asserts in this scandalous text for the "healers of souls," psychoanalysis is not the "cure" which enables us to escape from "civilization's discontents," to help humanity with its sufferings. For it is within this discontent, within this space—the space of civilization and history—that we are immersed, inevitably caught inside. We can, in effect, only transform it, and analysis is first of all the process of *critical transformation*: for this reason the discontent must be *practiced* to the fullest, worked through thoroughly.

But if analysis isn't the healing of souls, neither is it the glorification of the repressed, of that which has been rejected by both individuals and cultures as a whole. The point is not to counterpose to the discontent and its "incurability" another space, a dimension of truth that the reigning powers had hidden. The repressed must play its game, its role, within the space that rejected it. This is the "unbearable" impact of psychoanalysis: because here it is the rules of exclusion themselves that are called into question, the rules of dominion and the logic of dominion.

The two ways described here—those of the cure and of negative alterity—were already present in classical culture, in Freud's Goethe of Freud, in the culture that Freud radically called into question without ever explicitly opposing. Before the world of *Vergänglichkeit*, of the transient and precarious, before the world that is only a "sign," Goethe "demonstrates" the solution of Mephistopheles: this sign, the sign of what passes away, "spins in a circle as if it really existed. I'll take eternal emptiness instead."[50] And he demonstrates as well how this condition is overcome through an *askesis* in which the "indescribability" of precariousness achieves fulfillment: it is the destiny of Faust in the process of recomposition in which "salvation and tragedy, life and death, become one."[51] Or, if we wish—in a more bourgeois spirit—it is the theme (and destiny) of renunciation that runs throughout the *Elective Affinities*.

But if the Faustian *askesis* had become manifestly impracticable in the crisis that Freud moves within, it is just this impracticability that gives rise to its opposite, to the great negative perspective of Mephistopheles. It is the tragic dimension (the enchantment of crisis and discontent) of Kraus, the "silence" of Hofmannsthal's Lord Chandos, the farewell of Mahler's *Lied von der Erde*. Freud's greatness lies in having rejected even this temptation of the tragic, negative recomposition of a lost totality,[52] which is what we find reconverted into a positivity within our critical space in the rhizomatic strategies of alterity.

It is therefore not negation that calls the logic of classical dominion into question. Such negation is rather entirely contained within its dominion. The rules, the laws, the discourses that traverse, move and speak the crisis are not those of the dialectic of totality and negativity. And it is only by practicing these discourses within the crisis that we can transform them. This is the choice of the "conservative" Freud, a choice that situates him decisively beyond (and thus within our space and time) the myriad minstrels of the negative, or the champions of a *naturally* revolutionary unconscious. It is the choice not to sublimate and not to negate the condition of precariousness and crisis *but to know it*. And this knowledge is not a *Theoria*, not a General Critique made from outside the crisis that unifies its diverse elements and somehow redeems them through its rigor.[53] Critical knowledge is constructed entirely within the space of crisis, incorporates the "motives" of its precariousness and risk; it has no foundation upon which to rest nor an end that guarantees it by connecting it to a hidden origin. In the face of the contradictory plurality of the real there is no *one* discourse that can comprehend it entirely because our discourses are themselves within the crisis. We cannot therefore explain reality, we can only describe it, elaborate it through "die Mangel unserer Beschreibung,"[54] that is, the incompleteness of our description which, as Freud writes in "Constructions in Analysis," is the "only interpretation of which we can be sure."

To know the crisis is thus not to assert an absolute alterity but to move through it, to negotiate and reconstruct its mechanisms through a long and difficult scientific *labor*. It is a "hesitating" path, then, which "makes no claims to being self-contained and to the construction of systems" which would finally constitute a surrender to the desire to solve "all the problems of our existence uniformly," translating them into a coherent Weltanschauung.[55] Only through this gesture of radical acceptance of the rules of the game, of the processes and relationships which cross our historical space, is it possible to change the rules of the game, to construct new orders. This is the note on which Freud ends his thirty-first lecture of the *New Introductory Lectures on Psycho-Analysis*: the process of "land reclamation" through which the ego renders itself independent from the instances of the super-ego, perfects it organization, annexes new territories of the id. "Where id was, there ego shall be": the ego becomes, constructs itself, controls the contradictions of the id. It is the process of civilization *within* "civilization's discontents," a process that passes through the deconstruction of the great ideological fantasms of the super-ego, through the shattering of the eternal, "petrified words" of which Nietzsche spoke.

It is at this level that Freud situates his critique of the avant-gardes, his suspicion vis-à-vis Breton's exaltation of the id as the "extreme remedy" to the ego's ills, as the place of desire and therefore the "state of Grace . . . that results from the reconciliation in a single being of all that can be expected from outside and inside." It is here that the full, complete word is born, Breton's "word without creases," the word that puts us "on the road of total comprehension."[56] The unconscious celebrated by the avant-gardes is in fact a substitute philosophy, an attempt to heal on another scene (that of the unconscious) the wounds of the spirit. And this is just the opposite of Freudian psychoanalytic practice. For such positions entail the postulating of a natural truth, the truth of the unconscious, to which one can return as to a happy dwelling-place, a homeland beyond the distortions of civilization and consciousness. Freud however demonstrated the impossibility of this regressive utopia. We cannot escape from this world, cannot go elsewhere. The *Heimliche* of the unconscious manifests its radical *Unheimlichkeit*: the plurality of dialects that constitute it and that must be spoken, shattering every illusion of a linear progression towards a natural truth. The unconscious, in fact, is not the lost truth, it is not elsewhere—it is there where it manifests itself: in the effects it has upon the signifying formations that we produce within the process of transforming reality or, as Freud puts it, within "our dependence on the real external world."[57]

The therapeutic effect of the psychoanalytic work therefore lies in the transformation of our relationship to the world, in knowing more and, thus, as Foucault has shown, in being able to do more in the world. Madness isn't a rupturing of the orders of consciousness that leads us into the heart of truth. This is out-and-out exorcism. Madness has its method too, its rules, by which it seeks to control both external and internal reality, but the control it offers is wholly inadequate and in the end it substitutes hallucinatory forms for the reality that we do not succeed in controlling.[58]

Analysis is therefore constructed in that space within which the ego "reclaims" areas of the id, liberating itself from its subjection to the instances of the super-ego. And this practice, though created through the "roundabout journey" of medicine, is above all a critical practice, critical, that is, of ideological formations:[59] in a sense it consists of a return to the problems of philosophy without philosophy, there where, as Marx puts it in *The German Ideology*, "philosophy loses its means of autonomous subsistence."

It is in this place and at this level that an engagement can occur between two traditions and discourses so different from one another as those of Freudian analysis and Marxist critique. An engagement that cannot but assume the form of a clash, a reciprocal transformation, and which certainly cannot resolve itself at the level of a simple integration of the two, or of a conversion of Marxism into psychoanalysis, as in the various "Freudo-Marxisms" that have appeared on the scene in recent years.

To situate Marx before Freud or, better, *after* Freud, means instead to interrogate "the most powerful conceptual framework for the interpretation of capitalism that we have had access to up to now,"[60] to investigate one of the highest and most significant levels of the neo-classical constellation of the logics of crisis. It means, in effect, to break up the space of "answers" that Marxism has provided us with so as to reconstruct the strategic questions which are at the base of the Marxist project and which today, in this process of reconstruction, remain absolutely central. In fact, such a reconstruction means first of all *to produce new questions*, new problems within the space of our crisis and transition. Marxism and Freudianism are not complementary, as "the countless tandem champions of contemporary ideology [would wish]: Phenomenology and Marxism, Freud-Marx, etc."[61]

Freud does not therefore provide Marxism with the piece of the theory of the subject that it lacks (as Sève would have it, for example),[62] and Marx does not provide Freud with the structural and economic framework in which to insert its family romances so as to reconstruct, together, a new General Theory which finally comprehends everything. It is rather their radical difference which reproblematizes for us today, within our space, the ensemble of terms with which they, in such different ways, represented and "worked" and, to be sure, "resolved" the contradictions that marked their historical space.

To affirm the *necessity* of Marx after Freud (or Weber or Wittgenstein) means to establish this engagement between them, to put to Marxism those questions that Marx could not even formulate, to bring to crisis a tradition that ended up closing off these questions within a dense, defensive web, within an ideological body. To bring this body to crisis, to deconstruct it, means finally to construct the spaces in which all those practices that had been excluded and expelled from this body like an illness, as forms of irrationality, can come into play with one another. And it is in this struggle, in this engagement, and not in an act of simple integration, that both the subject and all the instances and forms of rationality that have been produced in recent years by emergent social groups and classes (the "personal is political," the "theory of needs," etc.) play a decisive role. The stakes, once again, are political. To modify, to shift the limits of a tradition and a regime of reason is both the task and the stake in a struggle around power in which new subjects find a voice, act and transform reality.

3. The Freudian discourse represents one of the most radical moments of neo-classical rationality and is, at the same time, one of the moments most "resistant" to ideological reconciliation: both at the medical level, when we recognize that the illness is not an *other* to be exorcised but a social product to be interrogated, a sign off of which we can read the contradictions that traverse the subject and all the signifying formations that it brings into play; and also, as we have seen, at the more generally cognitive level, when we frame all the terms of the crisis within the ambit of scientific discourse and its precariousness. The Freudian discourse thus constitutes itself as a material knowledge, a knowledge which moves through things and which represents the effective relations and tensions within things. In this sense, if the Freudian discourse is irreducible to the unity of a single discourse (be it medical, philosophical, etc.), it is equally irreducible to a purely applied dimension, to the dimension of the individual psyche, as to other fields (psychoanalysis *and* literature; *and* Marxism; *and* aesthetics, and so on)—an operation that would presuppose on the one hand a stable and definite object to interpret and on the other an instrument, psychoanalysis, that is equally stable and definite to be applied indifferently in a variety of possible fields. And yet the psychoanalytic institution has, in the end, done just this. Psychoanalysis, according to this view, should in the first place be the analysis of the individual psyche, a kind of psychology of adaptation: *psycho*-analysis. Excursions outside the strictly psychic and individual realm are thus to be done by reducing the various fields of research to the dimension of the individual psyche, which then function as verifications of the efficacy of the instrument of psychoanalysis, of its therapeutic validity.[63] To reduce the complexity of a literary work, or of an ideological formation, to the supposed *simplicity* of the neurotic symptom brings with it a radical reduction of the transformative capacity of psychoanalysis as well. For Freud, the procedure of analysis moved in precisely

the opposite direction: it was to construct the complexity of a space that had been rendered "simple" and homogeneous by way of the defensive reductions of the subject and culture. Evidence, for Freud, isn't the solution to the problem but rather the problem itself.[64]

But this is by no means the only attempt to recompose Freudian analysis within the framework of a unitary logic. Alongside the therapeutic reduction of analysis there exists as well the attempt to bring Freud into a "philosophical" dimension, so as to offer an account, through the new instruments of analysis, of Truth. Psychoanalysis would not thus be a practice of transformation which, breaking the "great stone" of truth, describes the contradictions that truth gathers into the fullness of a total word, but on the contrary the confirmation of the Truth through the discovery of the unconscious's enunciation. This attempt has a history and names attached to it: Jung, "Daseinanalyse," Ricoeur, Marcuse, Lacan. The work of Lacan is the greatest attempt to tear Freud away from the therapeutic reduction effected by English psychoanalysis and at the same time the greatest attempt to bring Freud into the sphere of classical philosophical discourse.

Lacan's attempt has had extraordinary success, especially from the late sixties onward. With Lacan or, better, after Lacan, we have been witness to a kind of psychoanalyzation of every discourse and above all of political discourse. And this, in my view, is the "problem" of his work: the problem of what have been the motives, the "reasons," according to which in the very moment that classical political discourse, heavily structured and homogeneous, seemed most intensively subjected to plural and dispersive pressures, the Lacanian discourse, which in reality reproposes an instance of radical recomposition, was able to impose itself as a hegemonic discourse in a wide social and political area that had championed just these dispersive pressures. After the publication of *Écrits* in 1966, which brings together two decades of psychoanalytic reflection and work, at the same time that these texts were being read within the context of new questions and needs, Lacan was drawing out this unitary tendency, this tendency towards philosophical recomposition, approaching in fact a kind of theology: the proposition in neat and decisive terms of every discourse's foundation in an ontological reality that transcends the real in each instance and that speaks, instead, to the "discredit" of the real and of real knowledge, to the "discredit of reason."

And yet Lacan's writings had been clear about this from the beginning. His aim was to propose "a *new order*, [that] means nothing other than a return to the *true science* whose titles are already inscribed in a tradition beginning with the *Theaetetus*."[65] This "true science" is the "pure way" that Freud had explored and that leads to "an immense truth" (*É.*, 527). The subversion of discourse, to which Lacan's readers "on the Left" have appealed, consists of unsettling discourse so that it can receive the truth, of which the analyst with his utterances and silences is master (*É.*, 313). The Other is "witness of the Truth," of that truth that is founded on the Word. In this sense the Truth is other from every historical association, just as the Word is other from every reality that might concern it (*É.*, 807-808). It is the old dream of Mallarmé, inherited by all the avant-gardes, of finding "un mot Total, étranger à la langue de la tribu." That word that Kafka said has "always been empty."

It is not my concern here to retrace the entire Lacanian itinerary, to show how his discourse is actually founded on the recovery of a certain type of idealism, on a certain reading of Hegel, of Heidegger, of Husserl, or of Lévi-Strauss or Koyré.[66]

My concern, rather, is to know why this project, and not others, met with success, became the discourse and sign for expressing a reality which is said to be foreign to this tradition. This success bases itself on the fact that Lacan radically assumed as given the precariousness of discourses, their impossibility of speaking the truth, mimicking this precariousness in his very style. Discourse, for Lacan, is never true, it is a *mi-dire* [non-speech], an imperfect, half-way speech, "vergänglich." And in this Lacan is fully within the space of our "discontent with civilization." But he represents, at the same time, an attempt to cure this discontent. In fact, our speech is imperfect insofar as only thus—through this imperfection, this "fallacy," this "lack of being" of the subject and its language—the truth can manifest its fullness. Certainly it is a fullness that is *other* from reality, other with respect to the real contradictions which are nothing but its medium. In this way the flight from the discourse of the logic of dominion ends up in a place which is in fact the morror image of that discourse.

Lacan's discourse interprets the crisis, then, but also the desire to evade its rules without changing them. And it is precisely from this point that the discourses of Deleuze, Guattari and Lyotard will set forth, whose work would probably not even have been possible without Lacan, in order to transform into a positivity what had been in Lacan's thought a tragic dimension. For the task of the analyst is that of opening the pure way of truth, yet this truth, in being other, possesses a "horrible" quality (*É.*, 868), and the words the analyst must pronounce, "I, the Truth, speak," are "unbearable" (*É.*, 867). But Lacan's discourse, even with its level of grandeur which is lacking in his followers', inevitably remains on this side of the crisis we live within and moves by way of a radical simplification of cognitive discourse, to which he attributes no flexibility or subtlety. Science is only the discourse of the "small letters," of desperate mathematization, to which psychoanalysis, insofar as it is a science, must have access.[67] The rest, incomprehensible to the small letters, is that which is marked by the great unsayable truth which, however, is "the cause causing every effect" (*É.*, 868) and which is therefore also the cause of the discourse that does not speak the truth: that truth before which one can do nothing save open oneself, yield. The Lacanian *béance* leads essentially to this, to a subject that becomes true in its impotence. And this knot is certainly not untangled by the Lacanianism of the Left, with its sermons on the subversion of the unconscious or on the revolution of the unconscious, that do little more than emphasize their distance from the truly revolutionary practices of real subjects that actually transform reality. In this distance the discourse of psychoanalysm can do nothing but pronounce the failure of the instances and needs that turn to it in order to speak and express themselves: in order to play a role in the world, not outside of it. The dialects of the unconscious are not to be heard in an amazed silence but, as Freud taught us, are to be transformed by a knowledge that is constructed through long critical labor. Only thus can they really speak and, through the construction of spaces that radically modify the rules, really affect the landscape of the dominant regime of reason.

4. The obscurity of Lacanian discourse, which is in fact the nearly mimetic clarity with which a discourse attempts to reproduce that which can only manifest itself in its precariousness and fallaciousness, has assumed an "auratic" value. Instead of being rejected, this discourse has apparently been claimed by everyone as their own, has been the discourse of the truth of all those who can only fully express themselves outside the rules and the law. Thus Catholic groups on the Right have read in it an appeal to a pre-capitalistic mysticism, an appeal to an "obscure God" beyond the region "of the dry climate of scientism" (*É.*, 289). Groups on the Left, instead, have found in it the expression of diversity, of an immediate and absolute alterity with respect to capitalist reality.

To criticize the system, as Deleuze and Guattari already note in their first work, *Anti-Oedipus*,[68] is to be a part of it. It is necessary instead to position oneself elsewhere with respect to the monstrosity of the capitalist *ratio*, in another space in which desire can produce itself and act freely without being constrained by the "molar" machines, the great machines of reason—the Freudian interpretative apparatus among them—within limits that would eventually strangle it.

Schizo-analysis, the proposition of Deleuze and Guattari, must liberate the unconscious from the great molar machines:[69] which is to say it must liberate the desiring machines. "Desire as a deterritorialized flux"—desire liberated form the great interpretative machines and rendered nomadic—"goes beyond labor and capital"[70] and constitutes reality itself: "the desiring machines . . . constitute the Real itself."[71] And in this Real, ideology does not exist, nor the necessity of analysis: once the confine has been broken through, once the flux of desire has been liberated, we have the pure chain-reaction of machines and pieces of desiring machines which *produce everything*, produce the whole of reality.[72]

Deleuze and Guattari propose a sort of liberatory "technology"[73] which constitutes a reality without depth, an unknowable flat sheet, insofar as "we know neither scientificity nor ideology but only chain-reactions."[74] And, in fact, for Deleuze and Guattari there is nothing to know because there exists no meaning. To become a rhizome, to expand without constraints or direction means "to act through forgetfulness and evasion."[75] One should not fight against the existing state of things. One should forget it and deny it because *it is not the true reality*.

Theirs is the edenic myth of the return to a lost happiness through the denial of the existant, to *that* true reality which one presumes the existant and its logic have distorted and hidden and which presents itself essentially and as the reversal of *this* reality that we live in. To the machines of technology, they oppose the machines of desire; to history, oblivion; to progress, underdevelopment and nomadism. And at that point where front and back can no longer be distinguished, they propose the grand myth of America which haunts the pages of *Rhizome*. The America without frontiers, the America of the "tramp," of the Indians, of "country," of Patti Smith: the America constructed in the mythology of American imperialism and through the process of almost limitless economic expansion. What, in fact, is more rhizomatic, more uncontainable, overflowing and uncontrollable than imperialism itself? What has more profoundly devastated the supports of the institutions of reason, becoming rhizome, destroying the past and memory, penetrating every space?

Certainly, faced with the destruction of the myth of linear progress proposed by Deleuze and Guattari, "we experience a healthy sense of disorientation," as Bodei writes, "before the complexity of the world and the plurality of possible ways to organize it cognitively."[76] "But," he continues, "we are unable to make a step forward," not only because of their repudiation of every modality of cognitively structuring the real, but also because their inverted image of things winds up getting confused with the things themselves; becomes a confirmation of the real, of the existant, just as it does not so much appear beyond analysis but, mythologically, before any analysis or act of transformation.

Body without organs, countless molecules dispersed outside of the territories of functional organization, all is indifferent: but, *ça marche*. This is the dimension of the Authentic, which the Freudian and Marxist "complications," according to Deleuze and Guattari, seek to distort within the great bodies of their theories. For them the battle to fight is first of all against these theories. Not against power, with respect to which they propose the dimension of *transversality*, a dimension that does not enter into conflict with power itself, which does not oppose it. One fights then against the theories that oppose power in order to transform it because in this opposition they contaminate one another, contaminate desire, forcing it into their webs.

It is curious that Deleuze and Guattari make Nietzsche work in favor of this affirmation of a desire *outside* the contradictions of reality, of this affirmation of a space that is *ailleurs*, elsewhere with respect to the "city" we live in. Zarathustra does not stop in front of the city, it is Zarathustra's ape that tries to stop him at the gate: "O Zarathustra, here is the great city; here you could find nothing and lose everything. . . . Rather spit on the city gate and turn back." Zarathustra does not walk away. The ape's appeal even spoils his praise of folly. One cannot turn back. One can only go through. Go through or remain prisoner of the city and of its lacerations.[77]

5. The thematics of desire, which inhabits the space opened by Lacan through the reduction of the complexity of the Freudian analytic practice to the Truth of which the Other is witness, finds more rigorous treatment in an author who, less well-known in Italy than Deleuze and Guattari, has in fact attempted to propose an "economy" of it: the economy of desire, the libidinal economy.[78]

For Lyotard there exists no stratification of the real which is, as for Deleuze and Guattari, a flat sheet, a film on which certain intensities appear, which can in no way be cognitively organized. Every theory is false, because "nothing comes from nothing, nothing is the effect of a cause" (*Él.*, 297). Our task is to "become sufficiently anonymous, sufficiently conducive so as not to arrest the effects" of these intensities which pass through us and run along the film of the real "so as to lead them to new metamorphoses, so as to exhaust their force of metamorphosis, the force of the effects that pass through us" (*Él.*, 207). To become better conducting bodies is to seek madness, which is that which is "unbearable in intensity" (*Él.*, 309) and which therefore produces new effects of driftage. This is the project of *Economie libidinale*. The negation of every message and every transformation, the affirmation of madness, which posit themselves as an "invulnerable plot, without a head, without residence, without programs, that spreads the thousand cancers of the tensor in the body of signs.

We invent nothing. It is already there. Yes, yes, yes, yes" (*Él.*, 311).

The conclusion is emblematic. Reality is there, has been there forever, immutable: we can only say yes to it. We therefore must be different, be mad, so as to better transmit the intensities that pass through us and upon which we can never act, that pass through this reality that we participate in, of which we make a "film" without depth or consistency.

Certainly, faced with these propositions we too experience a "healthy sense of disorientation." the liquidation of the illusion of a subject that sits in opposition to an object in order to organize it according to its laws calls our attention to the distance that separates us today from the classical cognitive strategies. But in this plural world in which the classical strategies no longer function, in the distance that separates us from them, we must produce new cognitive and transformative strategies. "Chaos," wrote Rilke, "provided it does not last long, awakens in us the presentiment of new orders"; and, again, "we are never closer to a 'change' than when life seems unbearable even in the smallest, daily things."[79] The "auratic" enchantment of deviancy, of madness, of *pure plurality*, of chaos, produces instead degenerate effects at both the cognitive and practical level, on par with the most solid, exclusive police apparatus of monistic reason, of the reason that discards into the ghetto of the irrational all the practices that can put its established structure into question. One strategy is, rather, little more than the existant as it is, in governing the existant, displacing every *determinate* and *antagonistic* alterity, every real antagonism.

In this way Lyotard arrives *explicitly* at the denial of all "efficacy of the negative,"[80] the denial of every determinate difference, such that capitalism and socialism express the same "imperial folly" (*Él.*, 131). Political parties and trade unions are thus "repressed blocks," just as are "all the discourses and all the actions of protest or politics" insofar as they represent the refusal "to become echoes and to follow the changes of libidinal investment" (*El.*, 138).

The critique of the historical organizations of the working class movement, the critique of Marxism and its tradition, is by all means a task that cannot be ignored from the moment that we find ourselves before *different forms* of historical "socialism." It is not therefore simply a utopian longing, nor even a pure science of society or philosophy or critical theory that we are dealing with but various concrete strategies and *real* powers. It is this diversified and contradictory reality that we must take into account, and no ideological apparatus, however powerful and well-equipped, can avoid this confrontation, can displace this problem, which is essentially that of an historical space *after* Marx. This does not mean liquidating Marx, but rather construing a scientific theory of class society—of the actual, real powers of society—that Marx had begun to construct. To demand all the answers from Marx means to displace all the questions. Thus, this position of Lyotard's too could be, in some way, salutary, if it didn't immediately invert itself in a regressive utopia of minorities and subjectivism.

The social groups that are to substitute the traditional political organizations (the "repressive blocs") are "elementary groups," those who are listed in the official registers as "women, homosexuals, minorities, prostitutes, immigrants" (*Él.*, 147). Elementary groups, minorities, a "multiple" reality and for this reason, Lyotard writes, "ever singular," and which must remain so, must remain minority, *must remain ineffectual*, so as not to become an opaque bloc, resistant to the running of libidinal flows. The deterioration of political discourse reaches here its nadir: "That which politicians write off, behind closed doors, as the apathy of the masses, a decline in combativity, alienation, is something quite different. It is vigorous discord, if sometimes imperceptible within one political perspective or another, scarcely defined; and this discord does not pass from the leaders to the rank-and-file, but passes through all of them.

It leads us, in fact, into temporality. Wait, hope, struggle, organize yourselves, says the political voice. And the other voice: seize the right moment, the future is, *possibly* and not necessarily, in the present instant and not tomorrow; no voluntarism whatsoever, do what presents itself to be done, listen to that which wishes to be done and do it" (*Él.*, 149).

The discourse could hardly be more radical. Precariousness seems to reach a tragic level here, in this future that is only the present instance, and only as a possibility, as Lyotard emphasizes. But this denial of politics is itself politics, and it is guaranteed by that which wants to be done, which wants to be, and which we are simply to transmit, becoming its carriers and medium. Certainty comes from outside us, from elsewhere, and guarantees the greatness of the minority, the other margin in which we are to position ourselves and *remain*.

The explosive force that has expressed itself in these years through the political articulation of determinate needs[81] is thus to be engaged not as the organization of forces which, wanting to count, pose the problem of power, but in order to confirm their own "singularity," their own "elementarity," their own "minority" existence.

At this point, having done away with political discourse and struggle, the only "direct efficacy" left becomes the activity of RAF, but not insofar as the Baader-Meinhof group could express, even distortedly, a revolutionary tendency towards modifying and transforming the existing order, but insofar as it presents itself as a principle of disorganization (*Él.*, 152) and therefore as an opening, as the dis-articulation of the social body, out of which libidinal flows can pour.

The fact that Deleuze, Guattari and Lyotard liquidate Freud and Marx and other "names" as so many representatives of the police arsenal of the bourgeoisie is decidedly a minor problem. In fact it isn't the "names" that constitute the problem. The political problem is the fact that this "will to impotence," this "autonomy *from* the real" that these discourses express, has become the discourse through which a reality that is within our horizon has attempted to express and represent itself, a reality that passes through our actions, that is, in a word, *part of us*. To retreat into *our* political discourse, limiting ourselves to the act of observation, to the taking stock of this ineffability, this failure and this impotence is also the failure and impotence of our political discourse. In fact, either the "political" will succeed in saying this too, or it will be consigned to the same silence: not to represent, not to speak, to remain silent.

We can admire Wittgenstein, who chose to remain silent rather than put into play a discourse such as that of classical reason which can no longer speak the real terms of the crisis. But his silence today is no longer possible. From the moment that we attempt to construct new forms of rationality that are able to explain the new which is produced within our historical space (taking for granted, certainly, the risk of failure and the possibility of repudiating the result of our labors), it is necessary to speak, to say what *appears* destructive, other unrepresentable as well. This is, in my opinion, what renders the Freudian example more relevant and near us than that of the tragic representatives of the *Krisis*: to have obstinately continued speaking even in the face of that which presented itself as *unvorstellbar*, unrepresentable; to have continued the analysis, interminably, the process of laying bare and transforming the contradictions of the subject, of "civilization and its discontents."

6. Lacanianism and theories of alterity have had widespread success in Italy. The political movement of 1977 often spoke these languages. Such reception has been facilitated by the work of certain groups who have endeavored to propound these theories and, more rarely, to elaborate them.

It is not my intention here to draw up a map of these groups. This would in any case be an impossible undertaking, given the capillary diffusion of a "wild" psychoanalysm that resembles more an indefinite nebula than an interweaving of discussions and propositions, a nebula that has largely been expressed in bulletins and leaflets. An investigation of this space might well provide us with interesting findings, especially in their divergence from what we know about the "traditional groups" of Lacanianism in Italy.

One of the most active, early centers of Lacanian research in Italy was no doubt that of the Catholic University in Milan and the group "Communion and Liberation," beginning with the writings of Dalmasso and Contri (the Italian translator of *Écrits*).

Quite different (and heterogeneous) appears to be the group working out of the journal *il piccolo hans*, which has attempted to open up Lacanianism to questions of linguistics, politics, epistemology: in a certain sense to bring the great Lacanian philosophico-analytical body into collision with other discourses and other practices. Theirs is, then, a taking stock of the plurality of modes of reason which cannot be reduced to any *one*, even that of Lacan which nevertheless remains the journal's and the group's main point of reference.[82]

The group I wish to briefly examine here, however, is that of "Semiotics and Psychoanalysis," founded in Milan by Armando Verdiglione and active in various other cities. The motive for considering this group is certainly not due to the originality of the work they have produced in this field but rather because their work seems to me particularly "symptomatic" of the "discredit of reason" that Lacan announced as a provocation and that here is taken, quasi religiously, *literally*. "La materia freudiana," the essay with which Verdiglione opens the volume, *Sessualità e politica*,[83] does not limit itself to echoing Lacan's "Freudian thing," but becomes an outright statement of faith.

Lacan's idealism takes the form of a great philosophical act which institutes a contradiction between the tendency towards truth and the precariousness of the real. All of this, this complexity, disappears in Verdiglione's repetition, where the discourse of Lacan mixed with Deleuzian terms and phrases functions as the pure reproposition of the idea which *ipso facto* produces the real: "Grammar, in its *ideality*, constitutes itself in fact as a machine which produces 'reality,' the reality of the factory and of the family, of the psychiatric ward, of the prison as well as of the political party."[84] The quotation marks could lead us to suspect an element of caution: the fact that grammar (as "Law") produces institutions that articulate power's dominion over the real. This would be a truism with which we could even find ourselves in agreement. But this is not Verdiglione's point. It is the name itself that produces the real—even sex depends on the word and image: "Every zone is erogenous, like a node which originates in an aleatory point, in a semblance, in a body-semblance. For this reason the *imaginary* is a dimension of the word that cannot be eliminated: a dimension of its own, yet co-existent with that of language, of meanings. And *the word has no beginning*" ("Lmf.," 24). The word, then, has no beginning, it is the originary reality. In it coexist the imaginary and meanings, which in turn produce that which we call "real": the signifier with its law, its grammar; the imaginary with its body-semblance. Both dimensions depend on the word, on Logos, which is the origin of everything.

But how do these two dimensions coexist in the word? "The image marks the mendacity of the signifier, which takes form out of error" ("Lmf.," 24). On the other hand, not even the imaginary can remain undisturbed. It has marked the mendacity of the signifier and must pay the price of shifting towards allegory: "Allegory is that which, passing through the image, speaks of something else and otherwise, until it constitutes itself as a *semiosis of the image* within the wrap and volume of the letter, as a mark of the image's displacement of meaning in the [signifying] chain"("Lmf.," 24).

Let's try to see what this discourse has communicated to us up to now. We have, then, an originary word, that has no beginning and is therefore absent from history. In this word two dimensions exist, incarnating themselves in a reality which they themselves produce: the signifier which, operated by the image, reveals itself as "mendacity" and a chain of errors; and the image ("body-semblance," etc.) which is operated by allegory, "speaks of something else and otherwise," shifting, perhaps towards the truth of the word wrapped in the volume of the letter.

A drifting, a displacement of meaning. Interpretation can do nothing but indicate it, provoke further displacements ("Lmf.," 25). Besides, meaning belongs to history, and analysis has precisely to do with history: it leads us to believe, in fact, "that something is the product of contradictions," and "to start with contradictions is to start with meaning" ("Lmf.," 25, 27). We must therefore do without analysis which would lead us, precisely, to a historical banality, to the memory of struggles, of work, of practices that transform the real. But nothing is produced by historical subjects, nothing is produced out of meaning: "*I do not remember, therefore I discover*: it is here that something takes place in the word" ("Lmf.," 29).

We are rapt in a mystical *experience*—the displacement of meaning, the excess, the magical instant in which "something takes place," in the word of course—because we have already taken leave of the world and are arriving beyond, at the shores of the originary word which structures and contains everything. Even sex ("Lmf.," 32) is an attribute of the word; all of reality is an "accident" of its "substance." This word, so omnipotent and solid, despite the mendacity of the signifier and the displacement of the image, is the word of God. God is that which Verdiglione calls matter: "Matter is the practice that lives in its detachment, without a goal, uncomprehended . . . it produces a contraction or a split, it traces an articulation in the body, designs that border which cannot be related to the organism. Matter is *the dimension of loss*.[85]

At the same time the logic of matter, of this dimension of loss, "constitutes itself as the production of an impossible knowledge."[86] Matter is loss, then, something that comes from outside and surreptitiously introduces itself into the body,[87] is in the body but cannot be grasped or known because its knowledge is an impossible knowledge. But what is the body if it is something other than matter and organism. "The body is semblance."[88] Thus matter is not body: it is loss and this loss is unknowable. That which is body is not matter but semblance. And what then is semblance?

"The semblance is that absolute through which philosophy seeks its completion" and, further, "an object in flight . . . the corner irreducibly out-of-reach."[89] We are in an ever-tighter circle. Matter is loss and cannot be known; the semblance, in which this dimension of loss manifests itself, is itself an absolute and "irreducibly out-of-reach." Therefore matter is unknowable; the semblance of matter is unknowable: therefore we know nothing.

But wasn't there a specific logic to this dimension of loss which is matter? Didn't Verdiglione claim that "language is the logic of matter."[90] And that this logic, at least in its dimension of an "ideal grammar," produced reality, albeit in quotation marks? If it isn't possible to know matter and semblance, isn't it at least possible to know this logic and the effects it produces? No, such hubris is not allowed, because "there is no matter that is not language,"[91] and it is therefore language itself that is caught in the dimension of loss and unknowability. The space becomes ever more restricted. Matter and word are the same thing: are the *thing itself*. But the *excessus mentis* isn't over. If "there is no matter that is not language" one must further add that language itself does not exist, as

Verdiglione does citing Lacan: "le langage n'existe pas."[92]

We are thus before the void. And we approach this void with forgetfulness ("I forget, therefore I discover"). The true dimension of the event ("it is here in the word that something takes place") lies in its displacement from history, in the experience of the void, in the celebration of obscurity.

We are obviously not dealing here with the great Lacanian challenge to the truth. The affirmation of truth in Lacan presents a "terrible" quality insofar as it clashes with the space of the total inefficacy of historical languages. Certainly, these pages affirm the necessity of having the courage to do without the great word of Truth, but we cannot ignore the challenge that Lacan presents to the theory of knowledge. We may find his opposition between scientific discourse and analytic practice simplistic and irrelevant to the concerns of the moment, but we can't be sure that this *irrelevance* does not have a meaning, and even, as in the present case of calling into question the self-confident rituals of cognitive practices and discrete discourses, a capital one. To challenge these rituals even "irrelevantly" and tempestuously vis-à-vis their claims to truth can help us to recognize their internal temptations, the need for totality which inexorably runs through them and their *perspective*. In a certain sense we still need Lacan's discourse of Truth in order to measure our critical languages against the questions that Lacan's discourse opens within them.

Even the positions of Deleuze, Guattari, and Lyotard retain a certain function, at least through the "healthy sense of disorientation" that they provoke in us, through their insight into the real plurality that crosses our space. If we continue to be opposed to the more simplificative aspects of this insight, if we interminably continue to construct formations (however provisional) which control this plurality, which organize it in regimes of meaning, in strategies for transforming reality, nonetheless this insight continues to have meaning for us, continues to remind us that the analysis "hasn't said everything," that it cannot say everything. It continues to remind us that the analytic work is interminable, that plurality isn't a mere stylistic option but the result of the continual emergence of diverse social realities that must have their say. Even Deleuze and Guattari's affirmation of a "desiring" existence has a meaning for us, one that we must act upon, conflictually perhaps, but that cannot be suppressed.

In one way or another, all these positions situate us before essential questions, problems, real tensions. Not so with the celebration of obscurity and nothingness in the work of Verdiglione, whom I have considered as a *symptomatic* tendency within this space of the problematic. In Verdiglione we have the mere regression of discourse to a state of inefficacy, that discovers in this impotence and inability to say anything the exclusive, mystic dimension of its closure within itself, within its void. It is as if the great questions of Lacan found their closure here in a series of *theological answers*. The productive uncertainty which sets off processes of research and signification here become the totally unproductive certainty of the void.

This is the dimension, the site, where the confrontations cease. And it is precisely this cessation and closure that we must combat. In fact the affirmation of diverse, plural models of reason, the affirmation of the legitimacy of numerous, various discourses, does not signify an abstract principle of tolerance but rather the labor and practice that keep the spaces open where these discourses can clash with one another and exchange and transform their rules. And this is not a mere "linguistic game," a "game of logic," a "jouissance" of discourse and the word. To keep these spaces open, to keep these confrontations open, means to struggle so that just those social and historical realities that have not fit within the framework of classical reason and discourse can speak. Those realities have transformed and are now transforming that which we tend to call the framework of neo-classical reason: they are the new that prevents us from feeling definitively "at home" in the *gedeutete* **Welt**, in the world as it has previously been interpreted, and that force us to experience atopy [spaesamento] in the process of analysis which puts everything up for grabs once more, even itself and its rules.

This opening of criticism to the many faces of the real and to the complexity of their articulations and relations and mutations is not the institution of a critical super-ego,[93] a guarantee of the hegemony of analytic discourse—of a general critical theory—but is rather constituted by the practical and theoretical space which has been opened up by real struggles and confrontations, by the emergence of determinate needs antagonistic to the stable structures that are apparently all-inclusive and thus, in reality, violently exclusive. It also consists of the awareness that one cannot immediately step out of these structures into some mythical elsewhere and that the pure and simple negation of them consigns us to an impotent mysticism. Language, quite contrary to Verdiglione's theory of it, exists in a complex, material network of relations and functions. To work through language does not mean to propose new linguistic games, or not only this, but rather to work precisely upon the material network of relations and functions which constitute language and through which it speaks and represents the real.

At this point the "names" of Freud and Lacan are only signs of an engagement that is taking place within our historical space and that has as its objective the construction of a new relationship with reality. It is illusory to think that this objective plays itself out elsewhere, before or outside the city to which the madman wishes to block Zarathustra's way. The city must be passed through in order to go beyond. That this going-beyond is a struggle and that this struggle is *necessary* is perhaps the most significant thing that has emerged from the confrontation and collision between the Marxist and Freudian systems (and vast areas of negative thought). That the outcome of this engagement is anything but simple is as much as the great Lacanian "word" and the temptations of the rhizome have allowed us to understand.

The Foucault Apparatus

No special significance should therefore be attached to the name of the city. Like all big cities, it consisted of irregularity, change, sliding forward, not keeping in step, collisions of things and affairs, and fathomless points of silence in between, of paved ways and wilderness, of one great rhythmic throb and the perpetual discord and dislocation of all opposing rhythms, and as a whole resembled a seething, bubbling fluid in a vessel consisting of the solid material of buildings, laws, regulations, and historical traditions.

—R. Musil, *The Man without Qualities*

'Effective' history differs from traditional history in being without constants. Nothing in man—not even his body—is sufficiently stable to serve as the basis for self-recognition or for understanding other men. The traditional devices for constructing a comprehensive view of history and for retracing the past as a patient and continuous development must be systematically dismantled. Necessarily, we must dismiss those tendencies that encourage the consoling play of recognitions. . . . History becomes 'effective' to the degree

> that it introduces discontinuity into our very being. . . .
> 'Effective' history deprives the self of the reassuring stability
> of life and nature . . . knowledge is not made for
> understanding; it is made for cutting.
>
> —Michel Foucault, "Nietzsche, Genealogy, History"[94]

The Nietzschean "lesson" resounds profoundly in these lines of Foucault. It would seem that the eternal, "petrified words" have finally been smashed. No reconciliation is possible, "the history which bears and determines us has the form of a war," and the relations that are established within it are of the order of power, not meaning. The space of this history is thus a conflictual one, in which no "reason" can claim to shut down the conflicts which in fact constitute it. "*Homo dialecticus*—the being of departure, of return and of time, the animal that loses its truth and finds it again illuminated"—is "about to die." He who "was the master subject and slave object of all the discourses on man . . . dies beneath their chatter."[95] There is no longer any privileged point, a single perspective from which one can order events; there is no longer a sovereign discourse that can unify into a totality the multiple strategies that cross the spaces of history, penetrating events, organizing and dispersing them.

The "empty synthesis" of the I no longer holds together either. "One has to dispense with the constituent subject, to get rid of the subject itself, that's to say, to arrive at an analysis which can account for the constitution of the subject within a historical framework,"[96] for the subject is a product of history as well, a construction, a compromise formation: the result of a conflictual inter-weaving of instincts and of *their* thirst for dominion, as Nietzsche said:[97] the result of conflicts between the drives of the id, the ideological instances of the super-ego, and the instances that are dictated and produced by its impact with the external world and by the necessity of controlling it through representation, as Freud noted.

Nietzsche's *wirkliche Historie* and Foucault's "effective" history, their explosive force has broken up "the consoling play of recognitions," asserting instead how "the true historical sense confirms our existence among countless lost events, without a landmark or a point of reference" ("NGH," 155). The subject is one of these "events," and its genealogy can be reconstructed precisely through the historical plot of the clashes and conflicts and events that have constituted it, that have historically constituted the privilege which it has now irretrievably lost.

There is no nostalgia in Foucault for this loss. He is too Nietzschean to alleviate it with the promise or hope of "revolution and happiness; or revolution and another body."[98] There is no room for a theory of desire, for the idea of "a primitive, natural, and living energy welling up from below" opposed to "a higher order seeking to stand in its way."[99] Such a theory, according to Foucault, is internal to the organization, culture and history of the West and does not take into account the fact that "the law is what constitutes both desire and the lack on which it is predicated."[100] The theory of desire, however radical, resolves in a dialectical opposition the fundamental problem, that of the "positive technologies of power," the apparatuses and strategies through which *power produces*, produces even that which opposes it.

We do not therefore have an originary "truth" on the one hand and a set of apparatuses that repress, hide and distort it on the other. ". . . [T]ruth isn't outside power, or lacking in power. . . . Truth is a thing of this world: it is produced only by virtue of multiple forms of constraint. And it induces regular effects of power."[101] The struggle does not thus take place *in favor* of the truth but *around* it, which is to say around that "ensemble of rules according to which the true and the false are separated and specific effects of power are assigned to the true."[102]

What is at issue then is "a battle about the status of truth and the economic and political role it plays."[103] And it is here, according to Foucault, that the importance of Nietzsche lies: in having perceived and traveled the "aleatory path of truth," in having constantly questioned the dictate, "we must speak the truth," and thus in having attempted to construct the genealogy of the *need* for truth. The constraint to truth, the obligation of truth and "ritualized procedures for its production," says Foucault, "have traversed absolutely the whole of Western society for millennia. . . ."[104] This immense expenditure finds its explanation in the construction and accumulation of discourses that constitute the social body, but also in the apparatuses which exist to control it. Such apparatuses are guaranteed by the "discourses of truth," by the "potent effects" that they produce.[105]

It is the same problem that Freud had posed before the "extraordinary power" of the "conviction" of truth that has rendered the great ideological formations of society—and, at the microphysical level, the hallucinatory formations of the subject— "inaccessible to logical criticism."[106] Faced with this problem, Freud "chose" a critical labor of interminable construction-transformation, which finds its only support in analytic practice, and which incorporates within its very operation the possibility and risk of revocation. In fact for Freud, to demand certainty as a foundation would mean to "found" the analytic practice on unanalyzed values, to propose a "foundation" upon which "everything rests."

When Foucault places the accent on the "ensemble of rules according to which the true is separated from the false" and on the "politico-economic status of truth" he seems in effect to be *repeating* the great Freudian (and before that, Nietzschean) question, with an additional element which, in Freud's texts, was largely tacit: the fact that the question of truth is always tied to the question of power; that "knowledge . . . is made for taking a position" and that this position is situated in relation to power. But who knows? Who takes a position against whom? With what instruments? And how are we to socialize and control these instruments? And if the relations within a historical space are relations of power and not of meaning—if knowledge is produced by power and measures itself against power and not meaning— how are we to *negotiate* the meaning which nevertheless is produced and opaquely extends itself, or which articulates and diversifies itself around these relations? Doesn't skirting the question of meaning perhaps finally repropose it as an originary void beyond, instead of within, these relations of power? And doesn't this void of meaning end up transforming the world into an indifferent series of games without stakes, into a network of discourses, which had been the horizon and limit which the great thinkers of the crisis of neo-classical reason had come up against?

Power games.[107] This is Foucault's response. "Who fights against whom? We all fight each other. And there is always within each of us something that fights something else."[108] There is in fact no *outside* of power, and its micro-physics therefore passes through us.

2. "And yet isn't it perhaps necessary to condemn the seekers, philosophers as they may be, 'who go underground' and examine unexplored territories through cartography? I think of the work of Michel Foucault...."[109] No one more than Foucault, perhaps, has filled the map of the contemporary historical and epistemological space with the "new" genealogy of a series of disciplines through which power articulates its strategies. His is a "sounding of a complex territory," as Foucault himself says with regard to the *History of Sexuality*, a work which aspires "to correct itself as it develops, open to the reactions it provokes, to the conjunctures it encounters, and perhaps to new hypotheses."[110] A "diffuse and mutable work," then, itself a territory to be explored in its openness

to "contingencies," in the questions that constitute it but also in the answers that it offers.

In the cartography mapped out by Foucault we do not find "signs," or "reality," or "truth," but *apparatuses* (*dispositifs*), which are:

> Firstly, a thoroughly heterogeneous ensemble consisting of discourses, institutions, architectural forms, regulatory decisions, laws, administrative measures, scientific statements, philosophical, moral and philanthropic propositions—in short, the said as much as the unsaid. Such are the elements of the apparatus. The apparatus itself is the system of relations that can be established between these elements.
>
> Secondly, what I am trying to identify in this apparatus is precisely the nature of the connection that can exist between these heterogeneous elements. Thus, a particular discourse can figure at one time as the program of an institution, and at another it can function as a means of justifying or masking a practice which itself remains silent, or as a secondary re-interpretation of this practice, opening out for it a new field of rationality. In short, between these elements, whether discursive or non-discursive, there is a sort of interplay of shifts of position and modifications of function which can also vary very widely.
>
> Thirdly, I understand by the term 'apparatus' a sort of—shall we say—formation which has as its major function at a given historical moment that of responding to an *urgent need*. The apparatus thus has a dominant strategic function. This may have been, for example, the assimilation of a floating population found to be burdensome for an essentially mercantilist economy: there was a strategic imperative acting here as the matrix for an apparatus which gradually undertook the control or subjection of madness, mental illness and neurosis.[111]

We are therefore dealing with apparatuses: not with sex, but with the apparatus of sexuality; not with madness, but with a heterogeneous set of discourses which cover, circumscribe and delimit madness; not with a knowledge but with a field of knowledge regulated by laws—an *episteme*; not with guilt but with a system of punishments.

But is it possible, by negotiating the apparatus, constructing its genealogy, to reach that *urgency*, that strategic imperative that produced and determined it? Or behind the apparatuses do we only find other apparatuses?

Interpretation, Freud said, is interminable. Nietzsche said: "No, facts are precisely what there is not, only interpretations."[112] And Foucault: "Interpretation has finally become an infinite task." But "if interpretation can never be completed, it is simply because there is nothing to interpret . . . everything is already interpretation."[113] Perhaps the function of the apparatuses is precisely that of covering over, of sewing up this empty center, this cavity that no interpretation, no cognitive activity, will ever be able to touch in that it only clashes with other interpretations. The silence of this empty center evades, in reality, every word and is barely reflected in the background of the discourses that surround and besiege it.

To discover this silence, to perform an archaeology of this silence,[114] one must first pass through the genealogy of all these interpretative strategies, pass through and reconstruct their discursive tactics. It will be at that point that the interpretation can achieve a sort of *complicity* with the silence, become a silence itself that echoes the void beyond the apparatuses. "What is in question at an interpretation's point of rupture, in an interpretation's tendency towards a point that renders it impossible, could well be something like the experience of madness. . . . Such an experience of madness would be the sanction for a movement of interpretation which approaches the infinitude of its center and collapses, turned to ash."[115]

This is the place, the point, according to Foucault, that was abandoned by Marxism after Marx, so as to establish "the reign of terror of the index" against the "infinity of interpretations." This is the place instead where we find Nietzsche. This is the place, finally, where a hermeneutics takes form "which folds over upon itself, enters the domain of languages which never cease becoming implicated in one another, this region which lies between madness and pure language."[116]

The experience of infinite and interminable interpretation is then in a certain sense the experience of madness itself, of that which the strategies of reason with its monologues, with its discourses, with its silences, wanted to imprison: silence, which is a sign of itself and nothing else, the truth without word and expression. If interpretation will never be able to say anything beyond the apparatuses, it will however be able to reach the point of rupture and silence that is the silence of "madness" that the apparatuses wanted to force to speak in their language, in the language of their regime of reason.

Because of this Foucault and his collaborators prostrate themselves before the "case" of Rivière, struck with astonishment: "the utter astonishment it produced in us was our starting point."[117] All the medical, legal, police and juridical discourses are the plural apparatus that was produced in order to respond to the urgency of this "white space,"[118] which remains beyond, untouched and untouchable by any apparatus, if it is still possible today to have "a sort of reverence and perhaps, too, terror for a text which was to carry off four corpses along with it. . . . We fell under the spell of the parricide with the reddish-brown eyes."[119] There is then a truth which the apparatuses have not been able to transform. Rivière's memoir "has lost nothing of its strange power of trapping any interpretation which has any pretension to be a total one." Its silence is still vivid and "we think we *have demonstrated* this in the course of our study; and if this were not enough, the very choice we have made in refusing to interpret it would be yet further proof of this contention."[120]

If this discourse resists "all reductions . . . to a given order of reason," and this "resistance" is demonstrated precisely by Foucault and his collaborators' need not to interpret it and be instead accomplices of and subject to it, this is possible because such a discourse is *absolutely other*, something heterogeneous that the apparatus of power can enclose but never comprehend. This "white" space stands before the full and insistent buzzing of the loquacious apparatus. But the silence of Rivière and the voices of the apparatus never cross one another's path, do not contradict one another: *do not mutually transform one another.*[121]

It was just this space of transformation that Freud had articulated as the site of analysis. Foucault's discourse on the contrary must not interpret and transform, but push itself towards the experience of Rivière, to the point where "interpretation collapses, turned to ash." The aim then is to *re-state* the discourses of the apparatus in order to reproduce within its body—the body of interpretation—the white space that these attempted to circumscribe and silence, translating them into their own languages. It is the discovery of this white space itself which produces astonishment, which produces that neutral margin that is neither Rivière nor the apparatus, that space we tried to describe as "complicity" between the interpretation and the empty object that lies beyond the apparatuses.

The cartography of strategies and apparatuses therefore contains a white space, the impenetrable "heart of darkness" that is the ultimate *truth* of the cartography, its *meaning*. And if Foucault lucidly penetrated the plural and contradictory space left open by the crisis of the great modern philosophical apparatus, the dialectic, he stopped, however, at the edges of the "heart of darkness" of the "need" of the dialectic, he stopped that is in the same place that Nietzsche did. But, in fact, he stopped short of Nietzsche, from the moment that he posited in this "heart" the very truth of interpretation and of the discourses and techniques that have constructed themselves upon it so as to control it, performing a kind of recomposition on this side of the crisis, on this side of the will to radically transform its terms.

When Marlow penetrates the "heart of darkness" in Conrad's novel, he does not find the other, the different: he finds the labor and exploitation of Kurtz. When we penetrate the memoir of Rivière we do not find, as Foucault and his collaborators would have it, a being that "wandered for a long time, like a man without culture, an animal without instinct, that is to say, like something which, specifically, did not exist; a mythical being, a monstrous being impossible to define because it does not belong to any identifiable order."[122] This is, once again, the *myth of the other*. In Rivière's memoir we do not find absolute alterity, but rather a plurality of logics. Power, property, inheritance, family relations, the handling of money, his readings ("if I had even found a piece of paper for cleaning chairs, I would have read it"), writing, which is to say the *instrument* through which Rivière tries to articulate and represent himself, play a role which is both analogous and contradictory with respect to his judges.[123] We do not find alterity, but rather the contradictory circularity of culture: a determinate confrontation and struggle.

The "complicit" interpretation of Foucault and his collaborators in this case ends up being complicit with the judge, silencing Rivière yet again, enclosing him in silence and renunciation in a manner analogous to that of the medico-legal apparatus that attempted to silence him by translating him into its languages. To repudiate translatability as the resolution of contradictions and plurality does not have to mean setting up in opposition to the languages of power the other silence of the subject that is dominated by that power. It means rather making these languages clash with one another, so that, having broken the stone of the loquacious truth of the dominant apparatus, we do not find ourselves once again before the stone of the silent truth of that which is thought and spoken *otherwise*.

3. The apparatuses are "loquacious tactics," coordinated and governed by "great anonymous, almost unspoken strategies."[124] What can we read in this muteness? Is there perhaps another silence, besides the one we found in Rivière? Another, equally abysmal silence, which flows beneath and beyond every word?

There is in effect something that speaks through the coordinating tactics and strategies, something which has no voice of its own and which for that reason has been able to hide itself and confuse itself with the strategies and apparatuses that it deployed. Something that passes through both the minute tactics and the great strategies and that cannot be localized in any of them. Something that commingles with them, decomposing and recomposing them. It is the great silence of power.

Power speaks every language. It does not exist on its own, but only in the languages that it causes to speak, in the relations that it establishes: "Power in the substantive sense, '*le pouvoir*,' doesn't exist. . . . In reality power means relations, a more-or-less organized, hierarchical, co-ordinated cluster of relations."[125]

Thus "[power] is always-already present, constituting that very thing which one attempts to counter it with." For this reason it is necessary "to move less toward a 'theory' of power than toward an 'analytics' of power."[126] But what does this "analytics" say, what does it "represent?" Above all, a series of negations: power is not an ensemble of institutions, it is not a type of subjection, it is not a general system of domination, it is not an institution, it is not a structure, it is not a force, it is not something that one acquires, seizes or shares. There is an "omnipresence of power . . . because it is produced from one moment to the next, at every point, or rather in every relation from one point to another. Power is everywhere . . . because it comes from everywhere."[127]

Power, then, like the silence of madness, or the "white" space of Rivière's memoir that power has enclosed within its discursive web, cannot be defined. Both are silent, speaking only through a language which is other: speaking through the loquacious apparatuses themselves. Rivière articulates himself through the medico-legal apparatuses, and through these same apparatuses power articulates itself. One beside the other, mute, they mirror each other in the productive discursive practices, as one truth mirrors another truth on the *real background* of the apparatuses which they produce.

Not even in the great confrontations or great acts of domination do power and its presumed other antagonist speak directly, because "there is no absolute exteriority with respect to power," there is not power on the one hand and something which opposes it on the other, and the great acts of domination are "hegemonic effects" of the homogenization of local struggles. Class struggle, too, for example, is a *form*, a strategic apparatus through which power homogenizes the "infinite expansion" of confrontations. Besides, "there aren't immediately given subjects of the struggle, one the proletariat, the other the bourgeoisie."[128] Theories that homogenize the confrontations into an opposition of this type are in a certain sense complicit with the strategic project of power to contain local struggles. We must free ourselves of Marxism too, then, of the "Marx effect."[129] We must instead "recognize the indefiniteness of the struggle," "reactivate local knowledges."[130]

In a historical space in which life itself is a political object and in which "an entire political technology of life" has taken form, in which the mechanisms of power exercise themselves directly on the body, what can be proposed if not the indefiniteness of an indefinite struggle, if not the reactivation of subjected, local knowledges? Indeed the "the insurrection of subjected knowledges" must take action against the inhibiting effect of "global, *totalitarian* theories" like Marxism and psychoanalysis, knowledges that can only work locally once their theoretical unity has in some sense been "put in abeyance, or at least curtailed, divided, overthrown, caricatured, theatricalized, or what you will."[131] But what remains of this liberation of subjected knowledges, of this localization and particularization practiced against totality, if not an *explosive* and *healthy* effect limited to the sphere of solidified and petrified theories that have gradually taken on an inhibitive character? How can a local, particular knowledge oppose a power which is itself already local and particular—which is already micro-physical, already a political technology of the body?

The liberation of knowledges, this multiplicity of genealogical researches, is at once "a painstaking rediscovery of struggles together with the rude memory of their conflicts. And these genealogies, that are the combined product of an erudite knowledge and a popular knowledge, were not possible and could not even have been attempted except on one condition, namely that the tyranny of globalizing discourses with their hierarchy and all their privileges of a theoretical *avant-garde* was eliminated" ("TL," 83)

We cannot but be Foucauldean in putting into question theory as totality, its inhibiting effects, its internal hierarchy, from the moment that the real emergence of new social subjects has radically called into question certain fundamental concepts which had become *values*, thus radically reducing their practical and cognitive power. But the object of our critical labor is the construction of a material knowledge that can take account of, represent, the plurality of real relations, of relations of force, not an "anti-science" constituted one more time by the "brute memory of confrontations" on the one hand, and by the "meticulous rediscovery of struggles," a "learned knowledge," on the other. Such a "solution" not only doesn't bring us one step closer to the changing of the social mind, to the socialization and transformation of collective knowledge and power, but reinforces historically defined roles: the *content* of the people's memory and struggles, the intellectual's mandate to give a *form* to these memories and struggles. The proposition of the "indefiniteness of struggles" hides here the populist myth of immediate liberation. The word "liberation," in fact, recurs obsessively throughout Foucault's Lecture of 7 January, 1976, liberation until the "final battle" that would end the "political battle": that is, "only a final battle of that kind would put an end, once and for all, to the exercise of power as continual war" ("TL," 91). In these pages too, in fact, power remains invisible, and that which appears as the goal of the struggle for the anti-sciences are only the sciences. The battle is solely "that of knowledge against the effects of the power of scientific discourse" ("TL," 87). In fact, "if we have any objection against Marxism," writes Foucault, "it lies in the fact that it could effectively be a science" ("TL," 84) and is therefore an apparatus that produces the "minorization" of subjects and knowledges and is charged with" the effects of a power which the West since Medieval times has attributed to science and has reserved for those engaged in scientific discourse" ("TL," 85).

But is it possible to be "outside" of science and its effects, to be "outside," free from the subjection of knowledge in a myriad of knowledges that oppose it? Or isn't this the reconstruction of the dialectic against which Foucault fought in all his works? Doesn't perhaps the same Deleuzian opposition between oppression and liberation appear here? Between molar apparatuses and desiring molecules?

The point here is not to indict Foucault, undoubtedly the most stimulating thinker in recent years. Criticism is not a police apparatus. The point, rather, is to open a series of questions—alongside those already opened by Foucault himself—even there where he has offered answers. The point is to re-problematize his discourse, which is already loaded with problems and for this reason productive: to open within his text the confrontation, to accept fully the challenge of a work "capable of correcting itself as it develops, open to the reactions it provokes."[132]

4. As we have seen, Deleuze and Guattari's discourse tended to resolve itself into a sort of dichotomy of an "ethical" order: on the one side the molar body, the great organizations that seek to "imprison" and "strangle" desire; on the other, schizo-analysis that shatters the molar organization, that reproposes the diffuse molecularity of the body without organs, which is to say of the body without functional organization and difference, in which desire flows freely and proliferates rhizomatically. Foucault, as we saw, dispenses with the illusion of a desire that is other from power which in fact constitutes it within its mechanisms, rules and apparatuses. It is not a nomadic desire: it is power that organizes itself in strategies and dominations, that dissolves itself anew in micro-physical tactics, constructs its oppositions as the organization and control of confrontations.

Deleuze and Guattari negated history: in their analysis oblivion and forgetfulness are a flat surface in contrast to the stratifications of history. For Foucault, instead, it is precisely history, in the form of genealogy, that liberates knowledge. And yet it is not possible to do a history of power directly, but only through the spaces in which it exercises itself: a history of the heterotopias that it constitutes. But in this sense we could say that *all* space is heterotopic, a sum of heterotopias, the diverse and diversified localizations of the discontinuity and strategies of power. Outside of this there is only the non-place of utopia—that utopia which is in a certain sense *verified*, valorized, by the very discourse of deviancy which, once the capitalistic "deviation" is removed or annulled, should restore the naturalness of desire, of behaviors, of needs. In Foucault there is no discourse of deviancy, no dissidence, no nature outside of the organized spaces. There is nothing outside the interpretations of "knowledge."[133] And it is power itself that produces its knowledge: "Between techniques of knowledge and strategies of power, there is no exteriority, even if they have specific roles and are linked together on the basis of their difference."[134]

"Forms of subjugation and schemas of knowledge" are in fact inseparable, transmitting themselves together.[135] It is modern humanism that "makes the mistake of drawing the line between knowledge and power. Knowledge and power are integrated with one another, and there is no point in dreaming of a time when knowledge will cease to depend on power. . . . It is not possible for power to be exercised without knowledge, it is impossible for knowledge not to engender power. 'Liberate scientific research from the demands of monopoly capitalism': maybe it's a good slogan, but it will never be more than a slogan."[136]

Foucault thus makes a clean, salutary break with the regressive lamentations over science's dependency on power: power and knowledge are not only mutually implicated with one another, they *produce* one another. On the one hand we have a series of apparatuses, apparatuses of power that constitute the sole reality: we do not know sex, but sexuality, not madness but the discourses on madness . . . ; on the other hand we have a knowledge without which power could not exercise itself, could not exist. Similarly, neither could knowledge exist if it weren't through the power that presupposes it.

Here the great critical question of neo-classical reason is resolved: the fact that discourses represent and dominate the real, but only partially, only imperfectly, through provisional and revocable compromise formations. This was the product of the break-up of the great Hegelian system in which a translatability of the real into languages (scientific, philosophical, political) and their potential synthesis was instituted. For Foucault as well there exists a perfect translatability between power and knowledge:

between the real that is the ensemble of apparatuses of power and knowledge. There is no margin in which a critical process of transformation can be constituted and constructed. Power is entirely in its knowledge, it exercises itself everywhere in the visibility of its knowledge: the ensemble of heterotopias is thus united in the gaze of power. There is nothing to analyze, unsettle, interpret, and the recourse to the "emancipation of subjugated knowledges" here reveals all its weakness and inefficacy. What knowledge can we define as subjugated if, essentially, knowledge always generates power and power always presupposes knowledge?

Bentham's panopticon, so extraordinarily described by Foucault in *Discipline and Punish*[137] was based on the image of the center from which the gazes extended outwardly. In Foucault power has no center. The center is empty, and it is from this void that an open fan of perspectives, projected in infinite heterotopic localizations, spreads. But this empty center recalls another void, another "white" space, something that perhaps precedes, as Foucault writes in *Madness and Civilization*, every "seizure of knowledge": Rivière's memoir, the silence of madness that has hidden out so long, indefinitely, beneath the monologue of reason. The silence, this white space, lies outside every apparatus and knowledge, as does the empty center of power. And it is just this white space, that is not language and is not apparatus, that is the origin of every language and every apparatus, insofar as all discourses are produced in order to enclose it within the perimeter of words, to translate it into their networks, to articulate it within their technologies. And this is the point at which the pan-knowledge of Foucault meets with the non-knowledge of Lacan, it too originating in the Word of the other.

The monologue of reason, of which Foucault performed the genealogy in *Madness and Civilization*, becomes the infinite plurality of apparatuses, of which he performed the genealogy in *The History of Sexuality*. Both, however, lead to an archaeology of silence, of the silence that runs through the great anonymous and mute strategies and through the diverse and loquacious tactics. But, as we saw in our discussion of Pierre Rivière, the only archaeology of silence possible is that of astonishment, the "burning" and "subjugating" resonance that we are able only allusively to sketch out in the mise-en-scène and repetition of discourses and apparatuses.[138] In this mise-en-scène, at the same point and time, appear the silence of power and the silence of that which is absolutely not power. The apparatuses and the interpreter, their voice: behind their voice, power and madness.

5. The great attempt of the "hard Hegelian word" to legitimize the construction of spaces (full-blown "hieroglyphs of reason") in which contradiction could play its role without being destruction itself was definitively shaken by the great crisis of economy, politics and classical thought. It suffered a crisis because "the bourgeois world," which the contradictions "produce and exalt," was put into question by contradictions that could no longer be contained within this framework and within these orders.[139] This is what the great, by now classic, "dialects" of that crisis, from Nietzsche to Freud, show us.

Foucault is positioned within this critical and problematic space. He breaks definitively with a linear conception of history and forces us to measure ourselves against complex formations, no longer analyzable in terms of progress but of confrontation, of the interweaving of relations of power. But the outcome that we saw, beyond the genealogies, of the "white" space of Rivière and of power's silence also shows us how his thought too has certain effects, that for however open it may be, it too is an "apparatus" that responds to "a determinate urgency." Certainly, the system of "effects" of Marxism is not the same thing as Marx, but to size up its effects means to size up a formation that in some way produced them as well. To confront Foucault means therefore to confront as well the "apparatus" that produces him, the effects that it produces, often beyond his express intentions. That the extreme Foucauldean opening has also been a response to an urgent need for closure, the head of the *nouveaux philosophes* testifies: "It didn't take much to break up the Marxist conception of power and, eventually, the organized and coherent ensemble of the structure that it comprised. What is there in fact in common between these universally dispersed micro-powers, organized in subtle networks, substantially homogeneous, and the Power of the Marxists that was a system of gears, an articulation of instances, a set of disparities? Can one really still speak of separate and heterogeneous instances, one type determinant, the other determined, when one can see that the crumbs, the crumbs of power, are spontaneously positioned along the oblique lines that pass from one area to the next of the structure. . . ? Behind all the chatter of metaphors there is a new political philosophy that is being elaborated and perhaps with it a new political practice. . . . It is because knowledge and power are homogeneous realities that one can in practice serve as a substitute for the other. . . . The philosopher speaks, and for this reason itself he unsettles the order of the world."[140]

Certainly Lévy is not Foucault. But is Lévy's philosopher's word that changes the world really so far from the emancipation that Foucault wished to base on the union of erudite knowledge and the memory of hostile encounters? Is Foucault's ubiquitous dispersion of power so irreconcilable with Lévy's *naturalness*, according to which power orders itself *spontaneously*? Is the phantasm of Marxism that Lévy proposes totally different from Foucault's refusal of "Marx's scientific project," from the opposition he sets up between the science of Marxism and the anti-science of emancipated knowledges? It would no doubt be an error to impute positions to Foucault that are not his. But it would also be an error against Foucault and his problematic opening to pass over in silence the fact that his work has been translated into an apparatus that has given voice to positions that are regressive even with respect to the Hegelian consciousness of the "hieroglyphs of reason" and of the immense cost paid by the life of states and the life of the spirit for the control and domination of contradictions.

Yet certainly the greatest "urgency" to which the Foucault "apparatus" responds is not the distortion made of it by the *nouveaux philosophes*, when they call upon him to testify, despite himself, to the logos of truth embodied in the voice of the philosopher. The "discourse" of Foucault and of the Lacanianism of the Left—however different from one another—has become the discourse through which a real movement has spoken, a movement which calls itself powerful and unassailable in its innocence and its *autonomy*, a movement that calls itself "white," like Rivière, equally inaccessible to the apparatuses that would comprehend it in their languages: "In history there exists a *minor knowledge*, which actually eludes whomever challenges it on its chessboard of war. . . . Language which ceases to be representative so as to tend towards its extreme limits. . . . No historian will exist, we will allow no historian to exist, who fulfills a function that is greater than language, offering his services to the language of power, who reconstructs facts, grafting them onto our *silence, an uninterrupted, interminable, angrily extraneous silence. . . . A discourse without an object begins to speak.*[141]

We find here all the terms that we have examined in the texts of Foucault, we find his discourse, or at least the discourse of the apparatus that he constitutes: a minor knowledge, that eludes whomever; the function that is greater than language and is knowledge-power; the interminable silence of the one who opposes it. To one side is Rivière who "wander[s] for a long time, like a man without culture, an animal without instinct . . . a mythical being, a monstrous being impossible to define because it does not belong to any identifiable order"[142]; and to the other, the discourses of power, the "greater function of language," that seeks, precisely, without succeeding, to frame Rivière or the "facts of Bologna" within the order of a history that can be enunciated. The myth of alterity is at work here with a vengeance. The "discourse without subject" is located in a book that is "fragmentary, partial, a place without territory, an invisible city that slips under, that escapes from the rooftop, that is absent from the official mirrors." And it is in this way, through this fragmentation, that a "collective subject, foreign in its own city, organizes itself imperceptibly, changes terrain, side-steps the challenge of power."[143] And this myth functions precisely as the loser's myth of the innocence of non-power, or of the other knowledge, against knowledge-power: the myth of alterity against the dominant order of reason.

We are faced, once again, with the key problem at hand. And it is the problem not only of that which Asor Rosa has defined as the "second society," but is above all the problem that this "society" is unable to construct a real antagonism and that in order to speak it assumes these discourses. In fact, one cannot "sidestep the challenge of power," one cannot "elude the chessboard of war." We are *within* the confrontation, and such a confrontation can be won only by practicing it to the fullest, by radically transforming its terms. At this level autonomy does not exist. Nor does there exist an angrily extraneous silence, and this is certainly not the silence of one who *has been rendered mute*. The discourses of transversality, which should express silence and emancipation, in fact "proclaim with empty ceremonies their freedom in powerlessness."[144]

Certainly, Foucault's discourse is not only *this* ensemble of effects, which it nevertheless produces insofar as it is a discourse "of the border," and therefore extremely open, rich, problematic, subjected to tensions which pass through it and sometimes transform it. It is precisely because we are in the "urgency" that produced this discourse, because we want to make use of it, that we are lead to a critical analysis of it. And this operation, Foucault has shown us, is not pacific: it is the operation that opens within a theoretical space a terrain of struggle and conflict. It is at the same time Foucault's work's disposition to this conflict, its openness to the reactions it provokes, and its provocation of these reactions, that places it in such a central position within our historico-critical space. To interrogate it, to put it in question, does not mean to displace it but, rather, to affirm that we wish to make use of it.

Part Two . . .

Beauty's Ulterior Gaze

Beauty's Ulterior Gaze

> Beauty has no end in itself: for this reason it constitutes the sole end.
> —Simone Weil

I. An Erratic Movement

> Because it was only in later moments that I was able to love all that this sonata brought me, I never possessed it entirely: it was like life.
> —Marcel Proust

Jean-Paul Aron, in his polemical attack on the "maitres de penser" that have dominated the French philosophico-theoretical scene of the twentieth-century and, by ripple effect, European and North American culture during the last two decades, places at the center of this scene the figure and work of Georges Bataille. The beginning of Bataille's public activity was, in Aron's view, the "simultaneously discrete and explosive prologue to the intellectual history of the post-war era," while his death in 1962 provided this same culture with a monument with which to identify, in which to recognize its own "gratifying identity."[145] And yet, if we take the trouble to examine this "history," though we certainly find traces of his presence everywhere, in no place does it have real consistency: in no place can it be identified in a *decisive* manner. On the contrary, reconstructing the signs of this presence, and seeking to construct a plot with them—that is a history of Bataille's intellectual enterprise—we find ourselves before an erratic movement, out-of-reach, that presents us each time with its irreducible *marginality*.

Bataille was a philosopher, but a "dilettante," irreducible to any movement. He launched the great French school of ethnology, but never produced a study "in the field," thus leading Girard to write that his interest in anthropology was more of an aesthetic than scientific nature. He passed through surrealism, with a gesture of attraction and repulsion, of continual oscillation, that ensured his existence at the border of the surrealist enterprise. He took up economics, but in order to push his thought through a Copernican revolution, one that led him not only beyond the laws of economy but beyond the laws of thought itself. From the beginning of the 1930s (from "La notion de dépense" [The Notion of Expenditure] to *Les Larmes d'Éros* [The Tears of Eros], and thus for almost the entire duration of his scholarly life) he nurtured the ambition of constructing a general history of man and civilization, without however intersecting or dialoguing with the great French historical school of Febvre, Braudel, and Bloch of the *Annales*. He wrote novels, stories, poetry, aphorisms and, once again, we find ourselves before an *oeuvre* that literally has no place, no apparent location within French and European literary history.

If we pass from the cultural context to Bataille's texts themselves this impression of *atopy*, of placelessness, rather than dissolving in the *presence* of his *oeuvre* grows until it assumes the dimensions of an *enigma*. In fact, we do not find ourselves before that which is usually defined as an "oeuvre," but instead an immense accumulation of fragments, which appear not to be constructed according to any logic, unless it is possible to hypothesize a *logic of the fragment.*

2. Thought, said Plato, begins in astonishment.[146] But, as Heidegger wrote, "as soon as philosophy was in progress, astonishment became superfluous as a propelling force so that it disappeared."[147] It thus seems that no place is left, no form, no writing, that is able to catch the light of the gaze which, astonished, we direct towards things that seem to emerge in their infinite variety out of the indistinct; or that we actually turn our attention to our gaze which is directed at things, in a gesture that transforms the gaze itself into a thing, an object of our astonishment.

Not even to our *journal intime*, to our private and secret "Eckermann," do we say, as did Valéry, all that comes to mind, "and so much less/all that could come/if. . . ."[148]

Astonishment seems, then, destined to be drawn back into the realm of a "style," to be caught and frozen in the rules of literary, philosophical or scientific communication, relegating life and death, being and non-being, with their enigma that has stimulated us to *think*, off-stage or, at best, as Marina Tsvetayeva wrote, to the bottom of the page with an asterisk.[149]

If there is a form of writing (save the exceptional cases of Flaubert and Kafka where style itself constitutes the widest opening to that which is possible) in which *expectation* and *astonishment* for that which could happen if . . . endure, it is precisely fragmentary writing, which presents itself as an actual modality of thought.

I am not speaking of *aphorisms*, which, on the contrary, multiply and emphasize closure, proposing themselves as a totality, mutually reinforcing each other in their unshaken and unquestionable truth. The fragment is a typically "modern" modality, that seeks to gather the "pollen," the germinal states of thought, there where thought is open to the infinitude of the possible:[150] to the real as a plurality that cannot be contained within one concept or style. The fragment, then, already with Schlegel and Novalis, through Leopardi, Baudelaire, Nietzsche and Benjamin, forces itself into the interstices of "solely reasoning reason" so as to grasp the enigma of the thing: so as to enter the unknown space of the thing itself which is a continual oscillation between extremes, which is the arabesque in which the interweaving of differences that constitute the reality of our existence and of the world is designed.

3. Bataille's *oeuvre* is an immense fragment composed of a myriad of fragments. No exegesis that has tormented and at times obfuscated this text has succeeded in explaining why he published certain works, left others unpublished and published others still under various pseudonyms: why, for example, of the seven versions of "La notion de dépense" the particular one we read saw the light of day; why works like "La Limite de l'utile" were abandoned in their half-finished state; why, finally, Bataille presented even published works like *La part maudite [Accursed Share]* as fragments of a vaster work that projected itself into the future but that never was completed.

The publication of the *Oeuvres Complètes* in twelve volumes that has now been completed by Gallimard and that was to consecrate Bataille as a *classic*, has rendered this fragmentary logic even more evident, which must be our point of departure if we wish to have access to the sense of a *marginality* which, in Bataille, is the tragic awareness that the truth can never be contained within a system or an idea, but in the erratic movement of a search: in the quête of the *enigma*.

The world, writes Bataille, is given to man as an enigma. The book can only be the tale of the attempt to resolve or at least penetrate this enigma. At the time of *L'expérience intérieure*[151] Bataille believes he has found a point at which his various attempts, as we will see below, intersect with one another in a possible solution—the point at which reason and its other cross with one another in a possible vision of the real, which is precisely that of "La Limite de l'utile," which he was working on at that time. But actually "to have achieved this task" puts him before an invincible paradox. "To achieve" a sense of the world means nothing other than to discover that this achieved possibility, which by convention is called "reality," does not obliterate all the other possibilities but, paradoxically, confirms them. And it is at this point, as Bataille says, that he abandons the text he is working on in a fragmentary state so as to proceed, through another fragment, to "where man reaches the limits of the possible."

4. Nevertheless, these fragments, like the points of a strange constellation, circle around a single point, one sun, which sometimes, despite the explicit affirmations of Bataille regarding his appurtenance to a sort of solar cult, becomes the black sun of death: a resplendent darkness, erupting and sinking into the abyss, so that what is possibly the most fragmentary *oeuvre* of this century curiously becomes at the same time the most unitary, the most gathered in around its secret theme—an *oeuvre* of almost religious "perserverance."

Let us try to approach this centered center through what is perhaps (and the perhaps is obligatory here) Bataille's first book, *Histoire de l'oeil* [*Story of the Eye*], published in 1928 under the pseudonym of Lord Auch.[152]

The scandal of this work does not lie in its extreme eroticism, a kind of sexual hereticism which was quite *à la mode* during those years.[153] The scandal is truly in the *story*, in the *destiny* of the eye: in what it *sees at the end.*

The book moves through a series of simulacra of the eye (the eggs, the bull's testicles) that inexorably approach a site of invisibility, there where that which is *not* usually seen in the light of day will, perhaps, be offered to the gaze.

It is the terrible, final image of the *Story of the Eye*, the vision of the eye itself, of the eye that is seen: "'Do you see the eye,' she asked me."

... in Simone's hairy vagina, I saw the wan blue eye of Marcelle, gazing at me through tears of urine. Streaks of come in the steaming hair helped give that dreamy vision a disastrous sadness. I held the thighs open while Simone was convulsed by the urinary spasm, and the burning urine streamed out from under the eye down to the thighs below. ...[154]

The image is terrible and tragic. Terrible because it reveals the *death of the sun*, the metamorphosis of its light into a dead lunar glow. Terrible too because the eye, sunk within the vagina, where it was to find the truth that is not visible to the light of reason, through the opaque medium of the sperm and the transparency of the urine *sees nothing*: it is a dead eye, bearing witness only to death.

The image is tragic because here (and we will consider it more closely below), in the incandescence of an indelible symbol, it is possible, as in every symbol, to see its opposite. This death should thus be a testimony to life. But before this symbol becomes so transparent we will need to proceed further, further into the dark evidence of Bataille's work.

II. The Enigma

In the tables of Linear B we find many names of gods: approximately half of them, it would appear, lived on as Olympic gods, the other half was lost. We know nothing of them: they are pure names of the unknown, which appear alongside those of Zeus, Poseidon, Hera.

—R. Calasso

1. The eye sees nothing, not even itself while looking. It is caught up in the infinite blindness of death. And yet, as we just noted, this dead eye bears witness to a truth that has been at the center of thought and of every cognitive concern throughout human history: it is the truth of consumption, that truth which formerly expressed itself in tragedy in the assertion of life's total absurdity, or in the desperate *vanitas vanitatum* of Qohèlet. And despite the fact that philosophy, from Parmenides on, has exerted its best energies in an attempt to combat this non-being, in order to reassure us that non-being is *nothing*, is not an object of thought, philosophy has ended up protecting itself from this terrible perception through a sort of therapy: *apatheia*, the renunciation of the pathos of the world and of its vicissitudes, which transforms the life of the philosopher into a *xenos bios*, a foreign life.[155]

The evidence of this senseless waste remains before the gaze, inexorable and ineluctable. And it becomes that much more pressing within the modern epoch, when the infinite substitutability of things ends up bringing into *every* thing the sign of this death.

2. It is with this awareness that Baudelaire proposes De Maistre as one of the masters of contemporaneity, who uttered the most piercing words before what he himself defined the "terrible enigma:"

> Thus the great law of the violent destruction of living beings is always put into effect, from the most minute little animal to man himself. The earth, always covered with blood, is itself nothing but an immense altar on which everything that lives must be sacrificed ad infinitum, without moderation, without pause, until the consummation of the last things, until the extinction of evil, until the death of death.[156]

Let us not be deceived by the fascination with which Bataille is drawn to Aztec sacrifice: this is the formulation he has before him when, after the experience of the *Story of the Eye*, he turns to politics, that is to the attempt to give a viable meaning to man's life; this formulation, and that of science, which, with the Clausius-Carnot principle, asserts that the "arrow points towards increasing disorder, culminating in so-called 'thermal death,'" and that therefore "the time of thermodynamics is not reversible, for it tends to the degradation of all existence."[157]

It is also the reality of dissipation that closes Flaubert's *Sentimental Education* with a desperate exposition of tombstones, or Zola's *Bête humaine* with an inexorable rush towards nothingness, that wipes out his every bit of faith in progress. This is the inheritance that Bataille receives and which he attempts to shatter in *Critique sociale* with the essay, "The Notion of Expenditure," which forces revolutionaries, even heterodox ones like Souvarine, to distance themselves from him. It is at this point that Bataille's isolation begins, and, at the same time, his *necessity* within the cultural context of this century.

3. "Until the death of death." De Maistre's pronouncement goes well beyond an awareness of transiency. It does not even stop at the *athanasia* of *thanatos*, the immortality of death. This today seems to be the new frontier—reemphasized by science—of the tragic. Even the stars disappear in the sky of modernity and, with them, sunk in the same "black holes," seems to be the metaphysical tension that has forever urged man to the edge of darkness so as to seek the profile of another horizon beyond it, the emergence of another light.[158]

"'The Notion of Expenditure" is Bataille's first, still ingenuous attempt to overthrow this absurdity—the inexorable "normality" of this "evil"—turning it in a new direction, into an "evil" that is the inverse side of that evil. And it marks the beginning of the great theoretico-cognitive adventure which, from this moment on, will guide his every step.

It is, in a word, a matter of "reversing the principle of entropy," unsettling that which had apparently been assumed as unquestionable knowledge. And Bataille moves in this direction, against the science of his time, appealing to the ethnological science of Durkheim and to *The Gift* of Mauss, which provide him with the concept—that of *potlatch*—that enables him, at least initially, to think this reversal.

Potlatch is "the opposite of a principle of conservation: it puts an end to the stability of fortunes."[159] It is the gesture of expenditure, of *squandering* performed in primitive civilizations, which appeared to have no scope save that of establishing an act of *communication* through destruction. In this sense, the destruction of "useful" goods, rather than cause a fall into the abyss of nothingness opens up reality on two fronts. On the one hand this act of destruction actually annihilates the utility of the thing, offering us in the very moment of its annihilation that which goes beyond the useful and which, for the moment, we will call its "sacred character." On the other hand, this destructive act creates a space of communication, it too sacred, removed from the laws of exchange: of a communication which, again for the moment, we will call "total."

It is by radicalizing these positions that Bataille runs into the first aporia, causing him to return obsessively to this question, which at every step presents him with new aporias and which renders this itinerary and this story almost interminable.

4. In order to have access "to the insubordinate *function* of free squandering" man must invest himself in the inessential, yet necessary, *functions* of production: he must stay alive in order to squander; must produce in order to squander.[160]

To overcome this difficulty there is no recourse to science, to any science whatsoever. In a note written after a feverish night at the end of the 1930s, Bataille writes that the Carnot principle seemed to him a "clamorous absurdity: it proves by itself the infirmity that is connected to science,"[161] to every science, which is the most powerful mechanism of de-sacralization of the world ever conceived by man, which is to say of the reduction of the world to a heap of lifeless objects, with which there can be no communication outside of the logic of possession or use.

"La Limite de l'utile," fragments of an abandoned version of *La part maudite*, written between 1939 and 1945 (and that is while the greatest episode of collective destruction known to man was under way), was to have taken up just these aporias, overcoming the notion of potlatch with the "ultimate question": the "question of sacrifice."[162]

The "substance" of sacrifice takes us "precisely there where the enigma is situated, there where the key to every human existence is," which is to say into the heart of a "metaphysics" that illuminates the meaning of the "games that life has been forced to play with death."[163]

Only face-to-face with death in the act of sacrifice does one reach the maximum of communicable anguish: the dizzying dimension in which we are literally uprooted from our usual abode, from our frontiers and find ourselves before the other, open to it.

III. The Light of Evil

> God's sacrifice is creation: man's, destruction.
> —Simone Weil

1. In the notes and versions that multiply around "La Limite de l'utile," Bataille confronts the problem of knowledge. No longer

is there a theory behind him, like that of Mauss, or a "faith" to sustain him.

Sacrifice is at the origin of every knowledge, yet knowledge developed by separating itself from it: becoming objective, which is to say subordinating itself to objects. Clear and distinct knowledge "puts the known in closed vessels" and, "if one wishes to remedy the poverty of this isolation," says Bataille, repeating a great gnostic metaphor, "it is necessary to break these vessels."[164]

Authentic knowledge can be nothing but *experience*: it is an act of existence and of life, in comparison to which the Neo-platonic alternatives that have survived the advent of scientific thought pale. In fact, the moment I recognize the cosmos in the microcosm—the "sympathy" that makes of the object a part of me, the subject—I have in fact *reduced* the object to subject, the unknown to the known. True communication between subject and object takes place instead there where life reaches its maximum force, at the limit of death itself. But the very moment that we have access to this *limit*, the moment that we go beyond it, we enter the void, there where neither subject nor object exist any longer, nor communication between them.

Sacrifice sought to face this very limit, establishing between myself and the other a type of communication that touches the "sacred part, mine and others." But, when we arrive at true sacrifice, beyond its simulacrum, and thus when we make contact with *human sacrifice*, we are forced to confess "that for us this bond does not exist."

It is at this point, as we observed above, that Bataille abandons the project that can be associated with *La part maudite* in order to study, in *L'expérience intérieure* and in all the texts collected in *La Somme athéologique*, the various modalities of *dépense*—laughter, ecstasy, sacrifice, poetry, etc.—according to the "law of communication" that was to gather together in one place that which up to then had presented itself as separate or grossly confused: the knowledge of the object and the subject contemporaneously, within an experience.

2. Experience is "a voyage to the limits of human possibility," and its beginning is "non-knowledge."[165] The spirit is laid bare by the tension that breaks the rules of habitual knowledge. In this sense it is precisely nakedness without reserve that situates one before this possible extremity: before this absolute display that can no longer be spoken or articulated. Only the "sacrifice" of the word in poetry can perhaps find a form for an experience which otherwise would remain purely ecstatic.

The two terms that enter into communication enter a dimension which, on their own, they did not have, which annihilates them as separate elements, as *individualities*.

This annihilation of that which is separate is the irremediable wound that opens us to the other: to the other subject, to the world, to the "wind from outside." This "incurable wound of being" that offers us the possibility of reaching the "opposite of being" and therefore the *extremity of the possible*, is that which is usually called "evil," and which a sovereign gesture grants us in the supreme instant of love, of eros, which demonically, as Schlegel had said before, divides and shapes the world.

3. We will find all these terms as key words in the various re-elaborations of *La part maudite*, in its various articulations and developments.

That which rendered these words utterable was certainly the direct encounter with Nietzsche which, as we will see below, may well provide Bataille with the last word of his adventure. And yet even more decisive perhaps was the encounter with a name that has not yet been mentioned here and upon which all of Bataille criticism has kept silent, or said too little: I am referring to Simone Weil.

4. Bataille and Simone Weil are together in *La Critique sociale,* and their relationship seems to be marked by something that goes beyond antipathy: by a reciprocal incompatibility.[166] One of the great characters of *Le Bleu du ciel,* the greatest novel that Bataille wrote, if not in fact the only text of his that can be truly called a novel, is precisely Simone Weil, Lazare, for whom the protagonist declares that he feels an almost frightening sense of horror.[167] And yet the protagonist feels that he *belongs* to Lazare: he too, as they told him Lazare had done, stuck sharpened points into the flesh of his arms and hands so as to "inure himself to pain" (*LBc,* 442, 454).

Lazare is duplicitous, "perhaps the most human being I ever saw," and, at the same time, "a filthy rat" (*LBc,* 460). But this duplicity is the paradox of an "unspeakable communication," the more profound sense of a true communication which is theorized in this same period (at the beginning of the 1940s) by both Bataille and Simone Weil.

The basis for this communication is the wound, the laceration, and in this opening to the world and to the other there is the necessity of ripping things from the real order, from their poverty, and of offering them back to the divine. This is the task, Bataille will say in *La part maudite,* of *sacrifice.*[168] But this is also what Simone Weil states in *La connaissance surnaturelle,* where she writes that "sacrifice is a gift to God, and to give to God is to destroy."[169]

It is, then, in a gnostic dimension that Weil and Bataille encounter one another in a decisive and inextricable manner that will be in the end, as we will see, the solution to Bataille's otherwise paralyzing and unresolvable antinomies.

God, writes Simone Weil, abdicated by creating. Man completes God's work through a process of de-creation, which leads the thing towards nothingness, and we ourselves towards that uprooting, that atopy, that offers a different measure of reality. This gesture of de-creation, that Bataille will seek through the "names" of ecstasy and orgy, is precisely the limit of the possible, that impossibility that is the sole access to God. This impossibility has been called evil, and for this reason "we must love evil as evil" (*Q*, III, 109, but also 9, 71-73).[170]

IV. The Double Economy

> The tragic, an economy writ large.
> —Friedrich Nietzsche

> It is necessary for the will's energy to be dissipated in an irrecuperable fashion, so as to exhaust it entirely.
> —Simone Weil

1. In 1949 Bataille published the first part of what he himself calls his most important work, *La part maudite*.

In opposition to science, which freezes the real within its formulae, the kind of knowledge that this work proposes is that of the correspondence and communication between the ebullience of the real, its exuberance—which Bataille describes as Beauty with an exergue taken from Blake[171]—and the ebullience of inner experience.

Bataille shows, then, that he is on the verge of connecting the fragments of his work in a text which would present itself as a new logic of the real.

Economy is partial. It studies the productive processes, the processes of exchange, and finally those of consumption relative to the reproduction of the means of production. Economy "writ large," that which Bataille defines as economy in general, must instead also take on the dark, invisible yet ineluctable side of production: that which makes of economy not a common science but a tragic antimony. It is the paradox of excess, the fact that the maximum productive exuberance always corresponds to the maximum loss.

In this context Bataille reproposes the "ultimate question of sacrifice," that which, as we saw above, "de-creates" or "de-things" the thing, establishing a new relationship between subject and object. The victim of sacrifice is in fact the most "damned" because s/he goes beyond every possible order of things and reality.

Baudelaire, in one of the greatest essays of the nineteenth century, "The Painter of Modern Life," had found in an *excess*, in a "something more" incomprehensible within the laws of logic and nature, the possibility of grasping an otherwise inapprehensible truth. Baudelaire had given the name of "beauty" to this something more, which implies as well the *form* in which this "beyond" can be grasped and become the "thing" of an experience. It may be that Bataille, with his exergue, had this "truth" in mind which Baudelaire had described in its ineluctable duplicity. But in *La part maudite* Bataille remains tied to the notion of "evil." This allows him to navigate the shoals on which the "The Notion of Expenditure" had run aground, but not, however, as we will see, without other, greater difficulties.

2. Potlatch rarely attains the heights of sacrifice. It is an institution "whose significance is based upon the withdrawal of things from their productive consumption" but which does not liberate them from their enslavement as useful things, does not tear them away from the *order* and from their *poverty* so as to consign them to the *divine*. In fact, if squandering is in some sense opposed to the thing, "it takes effect however only by entering into the *order* of things, itself transformed into a thing." Even outside the limits of an archaic industry of luxury and sumptuousness, squandering is given its meaning within the order that establishes

social class, prestige and thus the hierarchy in which he who squanders is situated. Only sacrifice seems able to allow access to the intimacy of the thing, to its being, but for this very reason it must above all be the sacrifice of knowledge.

It is not possible, Bataille writes, to reach "the ultimate object of knowledge without dissolving knowledge itself." Only in nonknowledge, in the affirmation "I know nothing," is the void of the thing that is reduced to the status of mere object eliminated by the experience of the intimate oscillation that resides within things and which makes of them the site of infinite transits, infinite possibilities.

3. At this point *La part maudite* is interrupted by one of Bataille's true obsessions: universal history. He goes over the stages of civilization, as he would do in *Théorie de la religion*, in *L'Histoire de l'érotisme*, in *La Souveraineté*, in *Lascaux ou La Naissance de l'art*, in *Les Larmes d'Éros*, without going much beyond what seem rather summary and generic observations.

It is after having considered Islam, Lamaism, the birth of industry which leads to the exploitation of things to their limits, and Marxism which is at once the contestation and complement to it, that Bataille returns to the "ebullience" of the "accursed share," to the obscure meaning of a truth that he feels close to yet still out-of-reach.

The intimacy that sacrifice reveals in the thing, the full possession of this intimacy, is a sovereign act. The "accursed share" would be incomplete without analyzing this form of experience of the world too. And it is at this point that Bataille projects the second and third part of *La part maudite*.

But it is this notion of the ultimate "possession" of this intimacy that forces Bataille to rethink sacrifice itself. "Sacrifice cannot but posit a sacred thing. The sacred thing exteriorizes intimacy: it shows on the outside that which is actually inside" (*OC*, VII, 178). And what's more, it shows as outside that which is inside. *La part maudite* closes with the same aporia that had forced Bataille to interrupt "La Limite de l'utile": "There exists between my likeness and me a bond which touches the sacred part, of me and of others. This bond exists, but when a man is sacrificed," that is to say when one takes sacrifice to its ultimate truth, "we confess that for us this bond does not exist" (*OC*, VII, 542).

4. In *Théorie de la religion*, written at the same time as the published version of *La part maudite*, Bataille speaks of the "childlike unconsciousness of sacrifice," of the negative order (which is nevertheless an order) that sacrifice establishes. Only death emerges here as the greatest "disordering" possible, as authentic de-creation. But, with this, we return to the very heart of the enigma from which we started. If death is the only way to exceed the limit that constrains things to mere "thingness" and the "I" to being defined as opposition to this inescapable state of conditionedness, then there is nothing that can give meaning to the real, to its consumption, until the death of death. At this point there would remain nothing but suffering: the song of suffering. "That was all gods' work, weaving ruin there so it should make a song for men to come!"[172]

V. *Desire and Transfiguration*

> Absorbing all vital energy, carnal desire works in such a way that the rest does not exist, and therefore becomes one and the same thing . . . how to forgive the other for remaining other?
> —Simone Weil

1. In 1950-51 Bataille wrote the second part of *La part maudite*, which would go unpublished. It is *L'Histoire de l'érotisme*, which begins by decrying the limits of *La part maudite*: "I showed, by all means, that production was less important than consumption, but, consequently, I could not avoid revealing something useful in consumption (useful, too, and most importantly, to production)." The second volume, *L'Histoire de l'érotisme*, was to take much further the "general critique of ideas that subordinate," that lead to the "ruin of ways of seeing that are the foundation of servile forms."

This critique moves from an extreme experience of the possible, extreme yet still common to all men: the experience of eroticism, which is the "accursed share par excellence" (*OC*, VII, 9-13).

Eroticism cannot really serve any purpose and yet at the same time, in the transgression of mere animality, of sexual naturalness, it is the foundation of authentic humanity. Man is the animal that denies nature, rediscovering it however in his own excrement, through a gesture that is not mere dialectic negation (*Aufhebung*), because the oppositions do not disappear. There is not, in fact, an *overcoming* but rather a *transfiguration*: the curse is simultaneously the destructive and constructive work of de-creation and creation that grants us another nature, unsounded within the existing realm of concepts and facts.

Eroticism therefore puts us before the maximum corruption, in the place where the wound that cannot be sewn up or healed is opened. The wound that puts us face-to-face with death in the paradox of "horror and desire."

In the embrace, in the amorous and erotic hold, an unprecedented space opens up, where "we breathe an air that has never been breathed before," and where "the world appears in a new way."[173] For this reason eroticism has, perhaps, no limits. The desire that it expresses, and that expresses it, is always the desire of an other, of a beyond. "In a word, the object of desire is the universe in the form of him who, in the embrace, is the mirror in which we ourselves are reflected. In the most live instant of fusion, the pure splendor of light, like an unexpected bolt of lightening, illuminates the field of possibilities" (*OC*, VII, 100). Here, at the point that one discovers the most repugnant animality in the totality of being; here, in this terrible and joyous fall, resides the sense of an authentically tragic duplicity, which allows us to have the ultimate experience of death in the act of life itself. But it is, once again, Bataille's inability to think of the limit as a threshold that leads him towards a sort of catastrophe within his own discourse.[174]

The place of the embrace becomes, as we have seen, the "void in which there is no word," "a universe without limits or foundation" (*OC*, VII, 146). The control of this space is the *sovereign act* which is the absolute negation that anticipates "the end of history" and that consigns us to a present in which indifference and apathy rule (*OC*, VII, 163). Even the so-called "lessons of nonknowledge" of 1951-53 that Bataille was working on in the final days of his life affirm "the triumph of non-knowledge" within the perspective of "end of history."

But who can live outside history? Only the sovereign has access to this dimension.

2. This is the concern of "La souveraineté," written in 1953-54 as the third and final part of *La part maudite*.

Sovereignty is that domain beyond utility that all men can have access to in that *miraculous* instant in which they have the sensation of "dealing freely with the world" (*OC*, VII, 249). The sovereign in this instant, in the *kairòs* of this theopathic experience, truly feels that he is a god, experiencing the totality of contradictions of a limitless knowledge, which is the knowledge of the void. It is the instant in which knowledge ceases before the experience of that which is authentically essential, and which Nietzsche expressed with the terrible but nevertheless joyful cry of a happy subjectivity, because if God is dead man can truly become sovereign, master of himself.

But sovereignty is apathy, and apathy is exactly that which philosophy has always proposed as a defense against the world's vicissitudes.[175] Moreover, the distinction between the inesssentialness of instrumental reason and the essentialness of absolute knowledge is what philosophers have always preached, representing themselves with the *sovereign* image of a foreign life, a life which, extraneous to things that change, to the *pathos* of that which changes, posited itself in proximity to the divine.

Art proposes "to give some real form to subjectivity" (*OC*, VII, 404) which refutes the existing order of reality. And "La souveraineté" was to have concluded with an essay on Kafka in which Bataille wished to express "that which is principal."

Literature is the authentic legacy of sacrifice, in the sense that it destroys the habitual meaning of words. But it is also more than sacrifice in its disposition as an opening to the possible (*OC*, VII, 300, 408, 447-48, 456). And yet Bataille does not complete the final step that would have lead him instead to charge the "literary fiction" with an immense responsibility vis-à-vis a new and different knowledge. First he had to resolve the final, greatest aporia of his discourse: that which leads through eroticism, the accursed share par excellence, to sovereignty, and from there to stasis and stagnation—to the opposite of that exuberance that burst out like a cry from the frontispiece of *La part maudite*.

VI. The Look of Beauty

> Logos and Eros are one.
> —Simone Weil

1. The ebullient itinerary of Bataille's thought, the tangle of history and the tensions of the present mark out an intricate map that comes to signal a decisive turning-point. *L'Histoire de l'érotisme* went unpublished. Eroticism, the "accursed share par excellence," had not expressed everything that it had to reveal. It is in the 1957 version, entitled simply *L'Èrotisme*, that this un-said—that which Bataille had not been able to express—becomes acutely manifest, in the words that open the text and that provide it with its ultimate meaning, there where Bataille comes into contact with Nietzsche as never before.

"Of eroticism one can say that it is the affirmation of life even in death."[176] Or, put otherwise, *eroticism is saying yes to life even in death.*

2. Here the extremity of the possible is reached indeed, here where "being is put into question" at its very foundations with a "spasmodic joy," as Bataille writes in the final appendix of *L'Érotisme*, in *Les Larmes d'Éros*, Bataille's final text.

Bataille had often spoken of an experience that confronts death, of death generating life, which is itself the generator of death. Never had he reached the point, however, of comprehending death, dissipation, entropy, as themselves the shadow of life. The reversed negative had remained itself, even if overturned. It becomes something new when, as Nietzsche writes, we enter "the tremendous room of truth," there where we discover that "there is a happiness at the heart of things," which projects "its shadow around its lights."[177]

The "tarantula" that preaches the worst of possible worlds, seeking to find in them a reactionary motivation against the transience of existence, is defeated when we discover that "even that which we left out was woven into the fabric of every future; even nothingness itself is a weaver and master weaver." Bataille understands Nietzsche's "wisdom" when the latter declares that "if one day you can no longer endure life, you must try to *love it*" insofar as "the defender of life" is forced "to defend suffering as well." And in opposition to every "apathy," against every defense of indifference when confronted with the perception that everything fades, even the light of the stars, we must assert that "if a star has gone out and disappeared" its light "is still in motion. And tell me then: when will it cease to be in motion?"

3. Anchored to the Hegelian dialectic, pushing it to its limits, to the point of its dissolution and evanescence, Bataille had not been able to think the unthinkable, but only to *signal it*, through a tension exacerbated to the point of anguish of boundless openings, where one can only lose oneself. Bataille opened the Hegelian movement to the limits of non-knowledge, but for this space, which opens itself beyond reason, there was no possible word. Or at least Bataille did not find it.

For this reason Bataille turned to literature. But literature, subjected to a task that did not belong to it (that of philosophy's lieutenant) had ended up being flattened into a kind of *allegoresis*, which instead of opening onto a new sense of the real, enclosed it in a single meaning, in an image quite distant from the task, indicated lucidly once again by Nietzsche of carrying to "a unity the supreme tension of the multiplicity of oppositions."

The "guenilles" of Madame Edwarda's spread-open vagina remain just a "little piece" in comparison to that which this gesture should signify. Abbot C's little sack of shit. can signify the "accursed share" only through a flatly rationalistic gesture of forced equivalence, remaining forever beneath that which Bataille anxiously sought to express: that which the dead eye had instead allowed us to see with the duplicitous and ambiguous clarity of the symbol—not only death in life, but also, and perhaps more importantly, life which endures even in death.[178]

4. "Every true statement is an error if it is not simultaneously thought along with its opposite, and *one cannot think it simultaneously.*"[179] The dialectic solution of transforming contradictions into opposites to be mediated is only one image of a polarity that is instead constitutive in its irreconcilability of the real. But how to think this unthinkable?

Simone Weil, in her final reflections, intersects even more closely with Bataille's text, bringing it to an extreme level of clarity. We can grasp this unthought in a *form* and this form is, precisely, beauty, insofar as "the essence of the beautiful is contradiction," a "scandalous" contradiction, because irreconcilable.[180]

Reiterating the supreme manifestation of metaphysical tension in Dostoyevksy, Simone Weil tells us that beauty is not harmony.[181] It is rather dismemberment, insofar as it reveals the very essence of the real—beyond every attempt to comprehend it in a concept or idea—as contradiction, the place where opposites coexist and intertwine in an arabesque where all is present, nothing excluded, where nothing can be excluded if not by subjecting the real itself to the violence of an extreme will to power which reduces it to the disgraceful dream of rulers.

This supplementary energy, the "more" that Bataille had in fact sought to take into account in his historical surveys with a constant but unresolved tension to step outside of history is, writes Simone Weil, "Eros," the explosive desire "that we turn towards objects and that makes us love them."[182] This Eros that takes us into the very heart of things, into their intimacy, is a type of *reason*, is *logos*, even if it is a reason that takes us to a place where reason had never penetrated before. It takes us, precisely, into *atopy*, into the "absence of place" that gives us a different measure of the world.

5. "The world will be saved by beauty," Dostoyevsky had said. Proust, in *Le Temps Retrouvé*, had spoken of beauty as the

only form capable of holding together, in a frame of lights and shadows, of presence and absence, that which the intellect cannot give us, and which we nevertheless know is the profound meaning of our own existence. But no one perhaps went so far as Simone Weil in seeing in beauty "the apparent manifestation of the real," which is precisely its irreducible contradiction.[183]

No one went this far because this beauty as "dismemberment" and as "scandal" is, as Rilke wrote, terrible. And, in fact, Zola, in a novel that marks the awareness of the end of every aesthetics of Platonic or mimetic derivation, had understood in *Oeuvre* that the multiple reality of the modern is *unrepresentable* according to the canons of realism or with the usual languages. For this reason, in order to depict Paris he had presented the stupendous and terrible body, belly and sexual organ of a woman: because that which cannot be apprehended through the models of realism can be grasped only through an act of love: by Eros. But faced with the unknown of this beauty that becomes the vision of that which has never been seen before, the protagonist of the novel kills himself. Zola himself, though he had approached this truth, draws back, attributing Claude Lantier's obsession for beauty and completeness to his illness.

6. Beauty's ulterior gaze does not look at sex. It looks out, even in the *Story of the Eye*, beyond it. It looks towards the unspeakable happiness of a world in which everything takes place, in which nothing is put out of place. It is a de-situating gaze, insofar as it displaces the boundaries of admission and exclusion. But it is not, as Bataille thought for many years, limitless. Its trajectory itself designates a limit that passes through subjects and things: a *limen*, a threshold where opposites transit in new formations, tracing that arabesque that already Baudelaire had defined as "the most spiritual design," the "most ideal of all,"[184] because in it even the interrupted branches are present, even the abandoned

ways, which are always available for a new voyage, a future task.

7. Bataille dedicates a chapter of his *L'Érotisme* to beauty as that element of the object which marks it for desire. Taking up Baudelaire's extraordinary intuition, beauty here too is indicated as something ultra-natural, irreducible to mere abstract naturalness, to the *kata physin* that from Aristotle to Kant to Impressionism was posited as the absolute standard and limit of beauty itself.[185]. Even the sublime, which was to have caught that which escaped the confines of this category (of the *harmony* of a beauty *kata physin*), essentially confirms it: it denotes the work that exceeds the natural harmony by capturing, or trying to capture, our perception of the immensity of a nature that endures beyond the capacity of our forms, without however putting them in question.

In contrast, "ultra-naturalness" is not a dialectic "overcoming" of nature itself. It is nature caught in its opposition to that which is not natural: "Beauty, the negation of animality, ends up in the exasperation of desire, with the exaltation of the animal parts." And it is precisely human beauty which, in the extreme, incarnates this unthinkable contradiction. That Bataille should designate this excess, this beyond, as *profanation* (the way that Proust had traveled and gone beyond) certainly indicates a limit of his, but it represents more so the outer limit of his thought. Every consideration of his work must in fact begin from this limit which passes through it, illuminating it with a new light.

To be for life, to go beyond the meaninglessness of useless waste, to be beyond mere negativity in a gesture that recovers and reconstitutes a proper place for man, a new ethos for him, means to say yes even within death: it means to find a form in which life and death can coexist.

This is the intimacy with the thing that Benjamin recognized in Proust and which lead him to affirm that this was "Proust's greatest moral teaching," that he showed "*moins le revers de le monde que de la vie*,"[186] because if it is true that here, in this reversal, in this intimacy with the thing, we discover that "the sun of the cosmos is death," we also see that this sun attracts to itself "the lived instants, the gathered things," in a perspective that allows us to read that which has happened as an opening to that which has yet to happen: as the fruit of our love, of our fidelity to the thing.

Bataille's isolation reveals itself then as a proximity to a modern form of thought, which developed in the face of and against "the modern project" as a pure and simple development and management of forces. A thought which, fusing logos and eros, broke the great sacrificial chain of philosophy in order to find a *sophrosyne*, a wisdom of things that is a *pathos* for the world, which is at one and the same time a knowledge and experience of the world.

It is through his obsession with sacrifice that Bataille goes beyond sacrifice, towards that gift that is not simply dissipation but generosity, that same generosity that he had seen in Nietzsche, which is "on the side of those who give." For this reason Nietzsche's cry is joyful: "It is the cry of the happy subjectivity" (*OC*, VIII, 404). That which Bataille found in the end is a *new thought of subjectivity*, of a subject that spends itself, because only be spending itself can it conquer the horrible decree of that quotidian eschatology that erodes our appearance, our identity, our passion for ourselves, for the things and subjects that pass before our gaze.

Beauty is in the exuberance of this gaze, which negates nothing and embraces everything in its trajectory: it is the real overthrow of the decrees of an economy tied to the mere production of things, and to their simple, desperate and mortal consumption. The beauty that this gaze finds in the real, in things and in other gazes, can truly be the chance for the salvation that the world of ephemeral things awaits from us, we, as Rilke wrote, the most ephemeral.

●

Notes and References

1. This was of course the case in France as well, and it is sometimes forgotten that Foucault, who is often viewed as being antagonistic to Marxism, situated himself within this horizon: "It is impossible at the present time [1975] to write history without using a whole range of concepts directly or indirectly linked to Marx's thought and situating oneself within a horizon of thought which has been defined and described by Marx" (in *Power/Knowledge: Selected Interviews and Other Writings 1972-1977*, ed. C. Gordon, trans. C. Gordon et al. (New York: Pantheon Books, 1981), p.53.
2. The names of the authors in this series mark out some of the key reference points for the theoretical debates in Italy during the 1970s: Louis Althusser, Noberto Bobbio, Jürgen Habermas, Antonio Negri, Enzo Paci, Nicos Poulantzas, Rossana Rossanda, Mario Tronti, et al.
3. For a "'genealogical' reconstruction" of the contemporary Italian philosophical scene see G. Borradori, "Introduction," *Recording Mataphysics: The New Italian Philosophy*, ed. G. Borradori (Evanston, IL: Northwestern University Press, 1988]. This volume also contains an essay by Rella, "The Atopy of the Modern," which elaborates upon the theme of "atopy," which makes a brief appearance in *The Myth of the Other* and becomes increasingly prominent in Rella's work in the 1980s.
4. *La crisi della ragione. Nuovi modelli nel rapporto tra sapere e attivita umane* [*The Crisis of Reason. New Models of the Relationship Between Knowledge and Human Activities*], ed. A. Gargani (Torino: Einaudi, 1979) is in fact the title of an important collection of essays published shortly after *The Myth of the Other*. The book contains contributions by Rella, Bodei, Gargani, and Veca as well as by Nicola Badaloni, Carlo Ginzburg, Giulio C. Lepschy, Francesco Orlando, and Carlo Augusto Viano. This citation is taken from Aldo Gargani's introduction, p. 5.
5. With regard to the "flexibility" of the Hegelian model, irreducible to a pan-logism capable of encompassing the whole of reality, see R. Bodei, "Dialettica e controllo dei mutamenti sociali in Hegel," in R. Bodei and F. Cassano, *Hegel e Weber* (Bari: De Donato, 1977). See as well Bodei's essay entitled "Differenze nel concetto hegeliano di societa civile," in R. Bodei, M. Tronti, D. Boros, D. Zolo, *Società politica e stato in Hegel, Marx e Gramsci* (Padova: CLEUP, 197). See, finally, the typescript distributed by the Fondazione Giangiacomo Feltrinelli, *Ipotesi per un laboratorio politico—1978*, R. Bodei, "Proposte e domande." I have especially kept this last essay in mind, with which I am largely in agreement vis-à-vis all the questions taken up in this introduction.
6. Bodei, "Proposte e domande," p. 7.

7. Bodei, "Proposte e domande," p. 17.
8. Bodei, "Proposte e domande," p. 20.
9. Massimo Cacciari warns against the "myth of autonomy" understood as a "synonym for self sufficiency" in the essay "Razionalità e 'irrazionalità' nella critica del Politico in Deleuze e Foucault," *Aut Aut* 161 (1977). This issue is entirely dedicated to "Irrationalism and new forms of rationality" and should therefore be kept in mind with regard to this general debate of which only select themes are taken into consideration in these pages.
10. A. Asor Rosa, *Le due società. Ipotesi sulla crisi italiana* (Torino: Einaudi, 1977), p. IX.
11. The expression is Franco Fortini's, who lucidly examines this temptation towards an irrational resolution to the crisis in the various essays collected in *Questioni di frontiera* (Torino: Einaudi, 1977).
12. Bodei, "Proposte e domande," p. 17.
13. The constellation is immense and it is impossible to describe it adequately in an essay which aims to analyze only one part of it, one of its margins. It is worthwhile mentioning however the investigations that are closest to the present analysis, even if with widely varying positions amongst them, such as: the elaboration of the theory of needs done by P. A. Rovatti and the group associated with the journal *Aut Aut*; S. Veca, *Saggio sul programma scientifico di Marx* (Milano: Il Saggiatore, 1977); the work of M. Cacciari on "negative thought," such as *Krisi: Saggio sul pensiero negativo da Nietzsche a Wittgenstein* (Milano: Feltrinelli, 1976); the work of M. Tronti on the autonomy of the political; A. G. Gargani's discussion of epistemological rituals. These, obviously, are simply "names" that emerge from an extremely diverse and complex space which has, in turn, its story that needs to be explored.
14. "Now with every piece of knowledge one has to stumble over dead, petrified words, and one will sooner break a leg than a word." F. Nietzsche, *Daybreak: Thoughts on the Prejudices of Morality*, trans. R. J. Hollingdale (Cambridge: Cambridge University Press, 1982), p. 32.
15. F. Kafka, *Letters to Felice*, eds. E. Heller and J. Born, trans. J. Stern and E. Duckworth (New York: Schocken Books, 1973), p. 396.
16. Bodei, "Proposte e domande," p. 7.
17. A. Negri, *Il dominio e il sabotaggio* (Milano: Feltrinelli, 1978), pp. 70-71.
18. On the positions of I. Lakatos, see G. Giorello, "Programmi di ricerca, razionalita e progresso," *Quaderni della Fondazione Giangiacomo Feltrinelli* 2 (1978), pp. 15-16.
19. T. S. Kuhn's *The Structure of Scientific Revolutions* (Chicago: University of Chicago Press, 1970), while pointing out the puzzle-like character of scientific research, and the incommensurability of research paradigms, ends up organizing these paradigms in schemes and norms of regularity which only *at a certain point* break up in scientific revolutions.
20. See S. Freud, "Analysis Terminable and Interminable" and "Constructions in Analysis" (in *The Standard Edition of the Complete Psychological Works*, trans.

J. Strachey et al. (London: The Hogarth Press, 1981), vol. 23, the two great essays of the late Freud in which these themes are addressed most directly, though they occur throughout his work. On this point see section 2 of the following chapter.

21. Cf. *Scilicet 1-4*, trans. A. Verdiglione (Milano: Feltrinelli, 1977), p. 58; and *Écrits* (Paris: Seuil, 1966), pp. 282, 313, 868.

22. *Scilicet 6-7* (1976), p. 61. The "site" of plurality for Lacan is civilization, seen as a refuse deposit, "cloaca maxima," that exists in opposition to the truth which is itself non-contradictory. The "discredit of reason" is, inevitably, the discredit of civilization and history as well.

23. ". . . Theo-ry, is this perhaps the place for theo-logy in the world?" *Scilicet 1-4*, p. 77.

24. A. G. Gargani, "Scienza e forme di vata," *Nuova corrente* 72-73 (1977), p. 140; cf. also Gargani's *Il sapere senza fondamenti* (Torino: Einaudi, 1975).

25. A. Asor Rosa, *Le due società*, p. X.

26. M. Tronti, *Sull'autonomia del politico* (Milano: Feltrinelli, 1977), p. 19.

27. *Le due società*, p. XII.

28. L. Wittgenstein, *Philosophical Investigations*, trans. G. E. M. Anscombe, 3rd ed. (New York: Macmillan, 1970), par. 108, p. 46e; *Remarks on Frazer's Golden Bough*, ed. R. Rhees, trans. A. C. Miles (Atlantic Highlands, NJ: Humanities Press, 1979), pp. 7e and 10e.

29. M. Cacciari, *Krisis*, preface.

30. S. Veca, *Saggio sul programma scientifico di Marx*, pp. 41 and 44.

31. R. Bodei, *Proposte e domande*, p. 17.

32. S. Freud, *Moses and Monotheism: Three Essays*, in *The Standard Edition*, vol. 23, p. 122; *The Future of an Illusion* in *The Standard Edition*, vol. 21, p. 56.

33. A. Asor Rosa, *Le due società*, p. XVI.

34. S. Freud, *The Future of an Illusion*, p. 32.

35. *The Correspondence of Walter Benjamin and Gershom Scholem 1932-1940*, ed. G. Scholem, trans. G. Smith and A. Lefevere (New York: Schocken Books, 1989), p. 225.

36. G. Jervis, "Il mito dell'antipsichiatria," *Quaderni Piacentini* 60-61 (1976), p. 55. This essay (Now re-published in G. Jervis, *Il buon rieducatore* (Milano: Feltrinelli, 1977) offers an acute critical analysis of the temptation towards alterity within the discourse of psychiatry and also contains valuable observations on Lacanian thought which are of utmost relevance to the present essay.

37. R. Bodei, *Proposte e domande*, p. 2.

38. G. Jervis, *Il mito dell'antipsichiatria*, p. 55.

39. Jervis, *Il mito*, p. 55.

40. Or, in the extreme, in terms of "dominion" and "sabotage," as in A. Negri, *Il dominio e il sabotaggio*.

41. Cf. "The Dissection of the Psychical Personality," Lecture 31 of *New Introductory Lectures on Psycho-Analysis* in *The Standard Edition*, vol. 22. This citation is taken from the Italian edition, *Introduzione alla psicoanalisi* (Boringhieri: Torino, 1969). p. 477. The reference to the "many dialects" of the unconscious

is in "The Claims of Psycho-Analysis to Scientific Interest," *The Standard Edition*, vol. 13, p. 177: "But the unconscious speaks more than one dialect." The Freudian terms used in these pages in quotation marks occur throughout Freud's writings; I will cite specific texts only for longer quotations.

42. S. Freud, "Constructions in Analysis," p. 269.

43. A. Asor Rosa, *Le due società*, p. XIV.

44. This is Freud's great lesson in "Analysis Terminable and Interminable."

45. "Das Unheimliche" is the title of Freud's 1919 essay, translated into English as "The Uncanny" (in *The Standard Edition*, vol. 17). The translation of a term such as "Das Unheimliche," in which Freud invested a plurality of meanings, can only be approximative. It seems to me that the Italian term "spaesamento" [alienation, or, literally, "being away from one's homeland," or, as Rella now suggests, "atopy"—Trans.] is closer to the sense of Freud's text. Freud's 1919 essay is undoubtedly connected to the brief note he wrote in 1915, "Verganglichkeit" ("On Transience," in *The Standard Edition*, vol. 14) where it is precisely the sense of transience which produces atopy. On the term "atopy" see F. Rella, *Limina* (Milano: Feltrinelli, 1987).

46. Freud cites this passage from *Hannibal* by D. C. Grabbe—"Ya, aus der Welt werden wir nicht fallen. Wir sind einmal darin"—both in a letter of 30 July, 1915 to Lou Andreas-Salomé (S. Freud-L. Andreas-Salomé, *Briefwechsel* (Frankfurt a/M: S. Fischer Verlag, 1966) and in "Das Unbehagen in der Kultur" (S. Freud, *Studienausgabe*, Bd. IX (Frankfurt a/M: S. Fischer Verlag, 1974), where it appears, however, significantly altered: "Aus dieser Welt konnen wir nicht fallen." From *this* world we *cannot* escape.

47. Psychoanalysis, Freud writes in "The Moses of Michelangelo," "is accustomed to divine secret and concealed things from despised or unnoticed features, from the rubbish-heap, as it were, of our observations" (in *The Standard Edition*, vol. 13, p. 222). Carlo Ginzburg, in a essay of great interest entitled "Morelli, Freud, and Sherlock Holmes: Clues and Scientific Method" (in *The Sign of Three: Dupin, Holmes, Pierce*, eds. U. Eco and T. Sebeok (Bloomington: Indiana University Press, 1983)) sees in this attention to details the creation of a scientific paradigm based on "clues," common to the human sciences.

48. Cf., for example, S. Freud, "The Question of Lay Analysis," in *The Standard Edition*, vol. 20, p. 248.

49. S. Freud, "The Question of Lay Analysis," p. 253.

50. J. W. Goethe, *Faust*, trans. W. Kaufmann (New York: Doubleday, 1963), pp. 470-71 (vv. 11602-603).

51. F. Fortini, "Introduction" to *Faust* (Milano: Mondadori, 1970), p. XXIII.

52. I speak of Freud's relationship to this dimension, Faustian on the one hand, "Mephistophelian" and tragic on the other, in the chapter titled "Il tempo della precarieta" in F. Rella, *Il silenziol e le parole* (Milano: Feltrinelli, 1988).

53. This was, in a sense, Althusser's proposal, at least in *Reading Capital*, trans. B. Brewster (London: Verso, 1970) and part of what determined its success during the sixties.

54. S. Freud, *Gesammelte Werke*, Bd. XIII (Frankfurt a/M: S. Fischer Verlag, 1972), p. 65. Freud also takes up this theme in the sixth chapter of *Beyond the Pleasure Principle*.
55. S. Freud, *New Introductory Lectures on Psycho-Analysis* in *The Standard Edition*, vol. 22, pp. 182 and 158.
56. For these texts of Breton's, and for a discussion of surrealism, also in relation to Freud, see I. Margoni, *Per conoscere Breton e il surrealismo* (Milano: Mondadori, 1976).
57. S. Freud, *The Standard Edition*, vol. 22, pp. 174-75.
58. S. Freud, "Constructions in Analysis," pp. 266-68.
59. In the essay cited above, Carlo Ginzburg emphasizes the medical origins of the clue-based paradigm that takes form at the end of the nineteenth century.
60. S. Veca, *Saggio sul programma scientifico di Marx*, p. 95.
61. M. Cacciari, *Pensiero negativo e razionalizzazione* (Venezia: Marsilio, 1977), p. 95.
62. L. Sève, "Psychanalyse et materialisme historique," in *Pour une critique marxiste de la théorie psychanalytique* (Paris: Éditions Sociales, 1973).
63. What is done, to use a metaphor of A. Lorenzer, is that society itself is put on the analyst's couch; or the "genius" of the writer, or the philosopher, and so on.
64. For the problem of that which is "too clear" I refer once again to "Constructions in Analysis," and to my introduction to *Critica freudiana* (Milano: Feltrinelli, 1977).
65. J. Lacan, *Écrits*, p. 284. Further citations from *Écrits* will be included in the text in parentheses as *É*.
66. Lacan reads all these authors (and we could add Jakobson to this list as well) in a particular way that on the one hand reduces them to the role of precursors of the Lacanian discourse and, on the other, in this process of deformation, makes them speak of things with which they are not directly concerned.
67. This is the tendency in the final writings of Lacan, which emerges with particular force in the North American lectures published in *Scilicet* 6/7 (1976).
68. G. Deleuze - F. Guattari, *L'Anti-Oedipe* (Paris 1972), translated into English as *Anti-Oedipus: Capitalism and Schizophrenia*, trans. R. Hurley et al. (New York: Viking, 1977). Before writing this book with Guattari, Deleuze had a lengthy philosophical activity, with a series of works dedicated to Kant, Nietzsche, Bergson, which would allow us to reconstruct the philosophical origins of his later work. Most directly related to Deleuze's later problematic are the essays collected in *The Logic of Sense*, trans. M. Lester et al. (New York: Columbia University Press, 1990). F. Guattari is the author of a series of essays collected in *Psychanalyse et transversalité* (Paris: Maspero, 1972); translated into Italian as *Una tomba per Edipo*, trans. D. Levi (Verona: Bettani, 1974). Following *Anti-Oedipus* the two have published together a series of essays, including *Kafka: Towards a Minor Literature*, trans. D. Polan (Minneapolis: University of Minnesota Press, 1988) and *Rhizome* (Paris: Éditions de Minuit, 1976). I have taken up their work on

a number of occasions: cf. "Una tomba per Edipo" in *Aut Aut* 144 (1974) and the introduction to *Critica freudiana*.

69. Cf. G. Deleuze—F. Guattari, "Bilan-programme pour machines désirantes," in *Minuit* 3 (1973), p. 21: "In the first place, desiring machines are social and technical machines, but they are like their unconscious: they effectively manifest and mobilize libidinal investments (investments of desire) which 'correspond' to conscious or pre-conscious investments (investments of interest) of the economy, of politics and of technology in a determinate social field."

70. F. Guattari, *Una tomba per Edipo*, p. 389.

71. G. Deleuze—F. Guattari, *L'Anti-Oedipe*, p. 61.

72. Cf. G. Deleuze—F. Guattari, "14 Mai 1914. Un seul ou plusieurs loups?" in *Minuit* 5 (1973), above all pp. 7 and 11.

73. Cf. above all the "Bilan-programme," e.g., p. 18.

74. G. Deleuze—F. Guattari, *Rhizome*, p. 65.

75. G. Deleuze—F. Guattari, *Rhizome*, p. 71.

76. R. Bodei, "Proposte e domande," p. 13.

77. F. Nietzsche, *Thus Spoke Zarathustra*, trans. W. Kaufmann (Harmondsworth: Penguin, 1982), p. 176.

78. F. Lyotard, *Économie libidinale* (Paris: Minuit, 1974). Further citations from *Économie libidinale* will be included in the text in parenthesis as *Él*. Besides Lyotard's considerable writings on art, the following should be noted: *Discours, Figure* (Paris: Klincksieck, 1971); the essays closer to the problematic under consideration here are collected in *Dérive à partir de Freud* and *Des dispositifs pulsionels*, both (Paris: U.G.E., 10/18, 1973); "Petite mise en perspective de la décadence et de quelques combats à y mener," in *Politiques de la philosophie* (Paris: Grasset, 1976); and the older *Rudiments païens* (Paris: U.G.E., 10/18, 1977); and *Instructions païennes* (Paris: Galilée, 1977).

79. R. M. Rilke, *Briefe aus Muzot*. (Leipzig: Insel-Verlag, 1937), p. 163 and p. 103.

80. F. Lyotard, *Petite mise en perspective*, p. 125.

81. This is what has been proposed on the political front as the "theory of needs," or also the "need for communism," about which P. A. Rovatti has written on a number of occasions. See for example, P. A. Rovatti, R. Tomassini, A. Vigorelli, *Bisogni e teoria marxista* (Milano: Mazzotta, 1976).

82. An example of this kind of opening is the two conferences held in 1977 and 1978 organized by the "Freudian Practice," where S. Veca, M. Cacciari, F. Ottolenghi and others of a not strictly psychoanalytic background presented papers of a more political or epistemological orientation. My impression, however, is that we are still not so much on a collision course as on a manouevre of approach between the various discourses, that at the present time the discourses tend to complement one another rather than bring each other to crisis.

83. A. Verdiglione, ed., *Sessualità e politica* (Milano: Feltrinelli, 1975).

84. A. Verdiglione, "La materia freudiana," in *Sessualità e politica*, p. 23. Further citations from "La materia freudiana" will be included in the text in

parentheses as "Lmf."
   85. A. Verdiglione, "La sembianza," *Vel* 1 (1975), p. 5.
   86. A. Verdiglione, "La sembianza," p. 4.
   87. Cf. A. Verdiglione, "La scrittura del godimento," *Vel* 2 (1975), p. 44, where he speaks of the "intrusion of matter."
   88. A. Verdiglione, "La scrittura," p. 50.
   89. A. Verdiglione, "La scrittura," p. 50.
   90. A. Verdiglione, "La sembianza," p. 4.
   91. A. Verdiglione, "La scrittura," p. 46. It is surely quite incomprehensible why Verdiglione needs to distinguish matter from its logic and then go on to say that this logic is matter itself. But this is not the only loose end. It is also curious why he distinguishes an absolute word from a semblance, the body, which is then itself posited as an absolute. Or why he considers interpretation as an act of deterioration of that which is already in a state of deterioration. But we could continue at length.
   92. A. Verdiglione, "Significati istituzionali? *Vel* 3 (1976), p. 34.
   93. This is the suspicion E. Krumm expresses in "Davanti a un tribunale," *il piccolo hans* 15 (1977).
   94. In Michel Foucault, *Language, Counter-Memory, Practice*, ed. D. Bouchard, trans. D. Bouchard and S. Simon (Ithaca: Cornell University Press, 1977), pp. 153-54. In the French text as well ("Nietzsche, la Généalogie, l'Histoire," in *Hommage à Jean Hyppolite* (Paris: P.U.F., 1971), p. 160) Foucault puts the term *histoire 'effective,'* the translation of Nietzsche's *"wirkliche Historie,"* between quotation marks. Further citations from "Nietzsche, Genealogy, History" will be included in the text in parenthesis as "NGH."
   95. M. Foucault, "La folie, l'absence d'oeuvre," in *Histoire de la folie à l'âge classique*, 2nd ed. (Paris: Gallimard, 1972), p. 576.
   96. M. Foucault, *Power/Knowledge: Selected Interviews and Other Writings 1972-1977*, ed. C. Gordon, trans. C. Gordon et al. (New York: Pantheon Books, 1981), p. 117.
   97. See *The Will to Power*, ed. W. Kaufmann, trans. W. Kaufmann and R. J. Hollingdale (New York: Random House, 1967), p. 267: "It is our needs that interpret the world; our drives and their For and Against. Every drive is a kind of lust to rule; each one has its perspective that it would like to compel all the other drives to accept as a norm."
   98. M. Foucault, *The History of Sexuality, Volume I: An Introduction*, trans. R. Hurley (New York: Vintage Books, 1980), p. 7. I have preferred using the phrase "another body" based on the adjective "autre" of the French text instead of "a different body" employed in both the English and Italian translation.
   99. *The History of Sexuality*, p. 81.
   100. *The History of Sexuality*, p. 81.
   101. *Power/Knowledge*, p. 131.
   102. *Power/Knowledge*, p. 132.
   103. *Power/Knowledge*, p. 132.

104. *Power/Knowledge*, p. 66.
105. *Power/Knowledge*, p. 93.
106. It is in fact the great problem of the later Freud, to which I referred in chapter 1, section 2 of this volume.
107. "Les jeux du pouvoir," is also the title of an interview done with Foucault by J.-J. Brocher published in the *Magazine littéraire* 101 (1975), and translated into English with the title of "Prison Talk" (in *Power/Knowledge*).
108. "Le jeu di Michel Foucault, Entrevue avec Michel Foucault," *Ornicar* 10 (1977), p. 75; translated into English as "The Confession of the Flesh" in *Power/Knowledge*, p. 208.
109. This is the question posed by B. Barret-Kriegel in J.-T. Desanti, *Le philosophe et le pouvoir. Entretiens avec Pascal Lainé et Blandine Barret-Kriegel* (Paris: Calmann-Lévy, 1976), p. 180.
110. M. Foucault, "Prefazione all'edizione italiana," *La volontà di sapere* (Milano: Feltrinelli, 1978), p. 7.
111. *Power/Knowledge*, pp. 194-95.
112. F. Nietzsche, *The Will to Power*, p. 267. The more extended citation reads. "Against positivism, which halts at phenomena—'There are only *facts*"—I would say: No, facts is precisely what there is not, only interpretations. We cannot establish any fact 'in itself': perhaps it is folly to want to do such a thing. . . . Finally, is it necessary to posit an interpreter behind the interpretation?. Even this is invention, hypothesis."
113. M. Foucault, "Nietzsche, Freud, Marx," in *Nietzsche*, special issue of *Cahiers de Royaumont. Philosophie* 6 (1967), pp. 187-189.
114. An "archaeology of silence" is the program Foucault announces in *Madness and Civilization*.
115. "Nietzsche, Freud, Marx," p. 189.
116. "Nietzsche, Freud, Marx," p. 192.
117. M. Foucault, ed., *I, Pierre Rivière, having slaughtered my mother, my sister, and my brother...*, trans. F. Jellinek (Lincoln: University of Nebraska Press, 1975), p. X. Foucault's collaborators for the book were: J.-P. Peter, J. Favret, P. Moulin, B. Barret-Kriegel, P. Riot, R. Castel and A. Fontana.
118. Thus J.-P. Peter and J. Favret define the Rivière dossier ("si dur, si blanc") in their essay in the original edition of *I, Pierre Rivière* (Paris: Gallimard, 1973), p. 243.
119. *I, Pierre Rivière*, p. XIII.
120. *I, Pierre Rivière*, p. 250 (the essay is by P. Riot).
121. In *The Cheese and the Worms. The Cosmos of a Sixteenth-Century Miller*, trans. J. and A. Tedeschi (Baltimore: Johns Hopkins University Press, 1980) Carlo Ginzburg acutely describes the limitations of this work of Foucault's which leads, as he puts it, to an "irrationalism of an aesthetic nature," a "populism with its symbols reversed. A 'black' populism—but populism just the same" (p. XVIII).
122. *I, Pierre Rivière*, p. 195 (the essay, entitled "The Animal, the Madman, and Death," is by J.-P. Peter and J. Favret).

123. It is quite strange that neither Foucault nor his collaborators, caught up in the enchantment of alterity, payed attention to this dimension of Rivière's memoir. His inquisitors significantly insist on Rivière's readings.
124. *The History of Sexuality*, p. 95.
125. *Power/Knowledge*, p. 198.
126. *The History of Sexuality*, p. 82. Cf. also *Power/Knowledge*, p. 199.
127. Cf. *The History of Sexuality*, pp. 92-94; the citation is on p. 93.
128. *The History of Sexuality*, pp. 92-96; and *Power/Knowledge*, p. 208.
129. "Body/Power," in *Power/Knowledge*, p. 57 and passim.
130. *Power/Knowledge*, p. 57 and p. 85.
131. "Two Lectures," in *Power/Knowledge*, p. 81. Further citations from this text will be included in the text as "TL."
132. "Prefazione all'edizione italiana," *La volonta di sapere*, p. 7.
133. As Foucault explicitly writes in "Nietzsche, Freud, Marx."
134. *The History of Sexuality*, p. 98.
135. *The History of Sexuality*, p. 98.
136. *Power/Knowledge*, p. 52.
137. *Discipline and Punish: The Birth of the Prison*, trans. A. Sheridan (New York: Pantheon, 1978).
138. "Burning" and "subjugating" are the words that Foucault and his collaborators employ, cited above.
139. R. Bodei, *Differenze nel concetto hegeliano di societa civile*, pp. 37 and 41.
140. B.-H. Lévy, "Le système Foucault," in *Politiques de la philosophie*, pp. 185-186. It seems that the apparatus of the analytic of power is mobilized less against power than against Marxism. It is a position with which many diverse thinkers are in agreement, but all involved in the problematic of alterity: from the "Right" of the "new philosophers" to the Left (if, in this case, such categories still make any sense) with Deleuze, Lyotard, in part Foucault himself and he who appears to be his harshest critic, Baudrillard. Baudrillard goes so far as to say: "Marxism puts an end to the class struggle by hypostasizing classes and burying them in the theoretical enterprise." It is a strange power, this power of Lévy's philosophical word to unsettle the world; similarly strange is the one Baudrillard attributes to the theoretical word, to put an end to the class struggle. But that is not enough: it is necessary to push power into "its own death struggle" and that is possible only by challenging it "to be power, total, irreversible, without scruples and of a violence without limits" (J. Baudrillard, *Forget Foucault* (New York: Semiotext(e), 1987). This is a good deal more than irrationalism; it is to put oneself on the side of reaction.
141. AUTORI MOLTI COMPAGNI, *Bologna marzo 1977 . . . fatti nostri* . . . [Authors Many Comrades, Bologna March 1977 . . . our own business . . .] (Verona: Beltrami, 1977), p. 11. The emphasis in the text is mine.
142. *I, Pierre Rivière*, p. 195.
143. AUTORI MOLTI COMPAGNI, pp. 12-13.
144. M. Cacciari, "Il problema del politico in Deleuze e Foucault," in M.

Cacciari, F. Rella, M. Tafuri, G. Teyssot, *Il dispositivo Foucault* (Venezia: Cluva, 1977), p. 69.

145. J.-P. Aron, *I moderni*, trans. A. Serra (Milano: Feltrinelli, 1985), pp. 15 and 149. All citations from Bataille here will be taken from the edition G. Bataille, *Oeuvres complètes* (Paris: Gallimard, 1970-1988), in twelve volumes organized in thematic and chronological order (abbreviated henceforth as *OC*). The bibliography on Bataille is already of immense proportions—this too a paradox for a paradoxical author, praised above all for his "marginality"—and comprises by now classic essays by Sartre, Merleau-Ponty, Blanchot, Derrida, Foucault and Barthes. For the bibliography until 1975 cf. D. Hawley, *Bibliographie annotée de la critique sur Georges Bataille de 1929 à 1975* (Genève-Paris: Slatkine/Champion, 1976).

It is worth mentioning here a few more recent texts, most of which are listed in later bibliographies, such as D. Hawley, *L'oeuvre insolite de Georges Bataille. Une hiérophanie moderne* (Genève-Paris, 1978); M. Perniola, *Bataille e il negativo* (Milano: Feltrinelli, 1977); R. Sasso, *Georges Bataille: le système du non-savoir* (Paris: Minuit, 1978); A. Sarane, *Les libérateurs de l'amour* (Paris: Seuil, 1977); J. Baudrillard, *L'échange symbolique et la mort* (Paris: Gallimard, 1976); J.-L. Nancy. *La communauté désoeuvrée* (Paris: Christian Bourgois, 1986); M. Blanchot, *La communauté inavouable* (Paris: Éditions de Minuit, 1983); R. Ronchi, *Bataille Lévinas Blanchot* (Milano: Spirali, 1985); C. Pasti, *La favola dell'occhio* (Napoli: Shakespeare & Co., 1987); D. Lecoq and J. L. Lory, eds., *Écrits d'ailleurs. Georges Bataille et les ethnologues* (Paris: Éditions de la Maison de Sciences de l'Homme, 1987).

A biography, which is also an examination of Bataille's work, is: M. Surya, *Georges Bataille. La mort à l'oeuvre* (Paris: Librairie Séguier, Éditions Garamont, 1987).

Bataille's bibliography is a history of the traces that he left in the culture of his time, from the debates with Klossowski, Hyppolite and Jean Wahl, to *Tel Quel*, which begins its activity in his name, publishing those lessons of "non-savoir" that, were it not for his death, he was to have revised for publication as the journal's inaugural gesture.

Bataille's philosophical formation is essentially tied to Sestov, to his encounter with Nietzsche and to Kojève, through whom he became acquainted with Hegel and Cusano (the theme of death, of sovereignty and, with Cusano, of the "limits of the possible."

For the encounter with the "other" of economy and ethnology, cf. Lecoq-Lory, *Écrits d'ailleurs*; M. Eliade, *The Sacred and the Profane: The Nature of Religion*, trans. W. R. Trask (New York: Harper and Row, 1961), as well as R. Girard, *Violence and the Sacred*, trans. P. Gregory (Baltimore: The Johns Hopkins University Press, 1977), which asserts that, in places, Bataille's work "transcends the decadent estheticism of which it is the extreme expression."

The history of the relations between Bataille and surrealism is perhaps the best-known aspect of his intellectual activity, but consider at least: I. Margoni,

"Introduction" to *Per conoscere Breton e il surrealismo* (Milano: Mondadori, 1977). Bataille's political engagement begins with his collaboration with Boris Souvarine in *La Critique sociale*, who, along with the entire editorial board of the journal, distanced himself from Bataille upon the publication of "La notion de dépense." This did not prevent Bataille from speaking on numerous occasions of communism as the only movement worth engaging with, all the rest belonging irretrievably to the past.

146. Cf. Plato, *Theaetetus*, 155d; and Aristotle, *Metaphysics*, 928b-983a.

147. M. Heidegger, *What is Philosophy?*, trans. W. Kluback and J. T. Wilde (Boston: Twayne, 1958), p. 83. With regard to the themes of this section, cf. F. Rella, *Asterischi* (Milano: Feltrinelli, 1989).

148. P. Valéry, *Cahiers* (Paris: Gallimard, 1973), vol. 1, p. 16.

149. Cf. J. Brodsky, "Footnote to a Poem," in *Less Than One* (New York: Farrar, Straus, Giroux, 1986).

150. "Pollen," *Bluthenstaub*, is the title of a collection of thoughts by Novalis. Octavio Paz, with regard to the "logic of the fragment," writes, "I believe that the fragment is the form that best reflects the reality we live in, that we are. More than an isolated germ, the fragment is an erratic particle that defines itself vis-à-vis other particles" (O. Paz, *Corriente alterna* (Mexico City: Siglo XXI, 1967), p. 6).

151. G. Bataille, *L'expérience intérieure*, the first chapter of *La Somme athéologique*, in *OC*, V (translated by L. A. Boldt as *Inner Experience* (Albany: SUNY Press, 1988)).

152. *Story of the Eye*, trans. J. Neugroschel (San Francisco: City Lights Books, 1987) is not Bataille's first work, but that which begins his history and which for this reason is rightly and emblematically placed at the beginning of the *OC*.

It must be said, and we will turn to this point, that none of Bataille's literary works equals the symbolic power of the eye imagery in this book, insofar as they are conceived either as the direct translation of an otherwise unspeakable existential experience (his masturbation in front of his mother's corpse, about which cf. Surya, *George Bataille*) or as the allegorical manifestation of a truth discovered elsewhere, within the realm of philosophico-theoretical reflection. Bataille is perhaps the author of a single great novel, *Le Bleu du ciel*, translated by H. Mathews as *Blue of Noon* (New York: Urizen Books, 1978).

153. *Le con d'Irène* by Aragon is only one of the many obscene novels which proliferated at the end of the 1920s in France.

154. *Story of the Eye*, p. 84.

155. With regard to the philosophical "therapy" for the vicissitudes of life and the "ultimate concern" of death, cf. K. Heinrich, *Parmenide e Giona*, ed. and trans. M. De Carolis (Napoli: Guida, 1988). With regard to the "foreign life" of the philosopher, and the enigma of his extraneousness to the pathos of the world, which becomes, for example, the Heideggerian indifference before the victims of Nazism, see the illuminating pages of H. Arendt in *The Life of the Mind* (New York: Harcourt Brace Jovanovich, 1978). H. Blumenberg studied the metaphor of the "philosopher" cut off from the fray of the world as a fundamental figure

in Western thought in *Das Lachen der Thrakerin* (Frankfurt a/M: Suhrkamp Verlag, 1987). Cf. also F. Rella, *Asterischi*.

156. J. De Maistre, *Le serate di Pietroburgo*, ed. A. Cattabiani (Milano: Rusconi, 1971), conversation VII.

157. This citation on the principle of entropy is taken from J. Améry, *Rivolta e rassegnazione. Sull'invecchiare*, trans. E. Gami (Torino: Bollati Boringhieri, 1988), p. 28, who makes of it a metaphor for the absurdity of growing old.

158. The death of the stars is one of the themes that concerns Benjamin in his reading of the great poet of modernity, Baudelaire; cf. the "arcades project," published in Italian as *Parigi capitale del XIX secolo*, ed. G. Agamben, trans. G. Carchia *et al.* (Torino: Einaudi, 1985).

159. "La notion de depénse," first published in *La Critique sociale* 7 (January 1933) (there are however seven different versions of this essay), now in *OC*, I, p. 311, and translated into English as "The Notion of Expenditure," in *Visions of Excess: Selected Writings 1927-1939*, ed. A Stoekl, trans. A. Stoekl *et al.* (Minneapolis: University of Minnesota Press, 1985). The opening of this essay seems related to some of the themes taken up by Freud in "Vergänglichkeit," on which cf. F. Rella, *Il silenzio e le parole* (Milano: Feltrinelli, 1988). Heidegger makes of this thematic one of the fundamental "Stimmungen" of thought.

160. "La notion de dépense," p. 320.

161. *OC*, VII, p. 548.

162. The note in question is a part of the unpublished text of "La Limite de l'utile," but the theme of entropy is also present in "L'Économie à la mesure de l'univers" (in *OC*, VII, p. 10), and in general in texts connected to *La part maudite*. Let us try to list these. Besides "La notion de dépense," "L'Économie à la mesure de l'univers" and "La Limite de l'utile," there is the text itself entitled "La part maudite" which is contemporary with the writing of "Théorie de la religion," which is, essentially, an extension of the former (all in *OC*, VII). A second part of the *La part maudite* is the unpublished *Histoire de l'érotisme* and *La Souveraineté* (again in *OC*, VII), which was to conclude with the text on Kafka, which was instead taken up in "La Litterature et le mal" of 1957 (*OC*, IX). Also *Lascaux ou La Naissance de l'art* of 1955 is within the sphere of *La part maudite*, as is the reworking of *L'Érotisme* of 1957 (*OC*, X). Bataille's last work, *Les Larmes d'Éros* of 1961 (*OC*, X) is also an extension of the themes of the complex of *La part maudite*. We need also to remember that, on the literary front, the novel *L'Abbé C.* of 1949 (*OC*, III) is conceived as a narrative translation of the themes of *La part maudite*.

Finally, Bataille himself notes at the beginning of *L'expérience intérieure* the direct link (also physically direct: the notes for both works were in the same notebooks) with *La Somme athéologique*, and therefore also with the "conférences sur le non-savoir," and the themes inaugurated by the "La notion de dépense," with which the work of an entire life is thus set in motion with a determination reminiscent of that with which Canetti pursues the issues of mass culture, or Benjamin those of modernity in the immense register of the *Passagen-Werk*.

163. "La notion de dépense," pp. 263-264.
164. The quotations in this section come from the notes relative to "La Limite de l'utile" (*OC*, VII, pp. 532-548). The image of the "breaking of vases" comes from the Lurian heresy, central to Hebrew gnosis. God, creating the world, had hidden his light within some vases that broke. Thus the light fell into things and hid within them. De-creation, as we will see below with Simone Weil, can be called the gesture that opens the thing, that penetrates its interstices, in order to liberate the divine light imprisoned in its opacity. For these themes cf. G. Scholem, *Major Trends in Jewish Mysticism*, trans. G. Lichtheim (New York: Schocken Books, 1961); *On the Kabbalah and its Symbolism*, trans. R. Manheim (New York: Schocken Books, 1965); and G. Limentani, *L'ombra allo specchio* (Milano: La Tartaruga, 1988).
165. This quotation. as well as the one closing the previous section, is from *L'expérience intérieure* (*OC*, V, pp. 15-18, 266 and passim.).
166. On the relationship between S. Weil and Bataille cf. S. Pétrement, *La vie de Simone Weil* (Paris: Fayard, 1973), vol. 1, pp. 351-352, 422, vol. 2, p. 102 and Surya, *George Bataille*, pp. 176, 219-220. Their relationship apparently was one of a total incompatability which hid however a profound affinity or "complicity" of thought.
167. *Le Bleu du ciel*, 1935, published in 1957, now in *OC*, III, p. 445. Further citations from the novel will be included in the text as *LBc* with page numbers in parenthesis. This is the only novel of Bataille's to possess a true narrative dimension, and an authentically Célinian rhythm. It differentiates itself from Céline for its sobriety and economy of writing (however paradoxical this assessment might seem) which at times recalls Hemingway's *The Sun Also Rises*. All the other stories, as we will have the opportunity to emphasize, are caught in the trap of a barely-displaced autobiographism, lacking in irony, which either pushes towards an unintentional grotesqueness or is moved by the concern to transmit, as Dante would have said, the truth "under the veil" of the literary form, which becomes abstract allegory. One does not do justice to Bataille if one does not re-frame precisely those dimensions of his work that have been ravaged by exegeses enamoured of merely verbal transgression.
168. Pp. 61-62.
169. The citations from Simone Weil are all taken from works of the early 1940s, contemporary with the works of Bataille's examined here. These are her *Quaderni*, trans. G. Gaeta (Milano: Adelphi, 1982, 1985, 1988) which will be cited in text in parentheses as *Q*, followed by the roman numeral of the volume and arab page number; *La connaissance surnaturelle* (Paris: Gallimard, 1950); and finally the anthologies *Attesa di Dio*, trans. O. Nemi (Milano: Rusconi, 1984) and *L'ombra e la grazia*, trans. F. Fortini (Milano: Rusconi, 1985).

Bataille undertook a brief foray into the issues of gnosis in a brief essay of 1930 written for *Documents*, "Le bas materialisme et la gnose" (*OC*, I) which demonstrates a knowledge of the main chapters that Puech was beginning to work on in those very years. But gnostic themes are present throughout French culture, from Balzac to Flaubert, as I believe I showed in F. Rella, *Limina. Il pensiero e le cose* (Milano: Feltrinelli, 1987).

170. With regard to the abdication of God through creation, a theme of Hellenistic gnostic thought, and of Hebraic gnostic thought as well (think, for example, of the theory of tzim tzum) cf. S. Weil, *La connaissance surnaturelle*, pp. 168-69. With regard to decreation and uprooting, cf. *L'ombra e la grazia*, pp. 44-51. With regard to atopy cf. *Q*, II, p. 252).

171. "Exuberance is beauty"—this phrase of Blake's is the motto which opens *La part maudite* and which makes full sense only at the end of the work, with *Érotisme*.

172. Homer, *The Odyssey* (Book VIII, 579-80), trans. R. Fitzgerald (Anchor Books: New York, 1963), p. 142.

173. On the embrace as entrance into an unknown place, where one breathes an air never breathed before, cf. F. Kafka, *Das Shloss. Kritische Ausgabe* (Frankfurt a/M: Fischer, 1982), p. 69. It is worth remembering that the third part of *La part maudite*, *La Souveraineté*, concludes in the name of Kafka.

174. With Schelling, Schlegel and Novalis, the modern opens onto the aporia of the limitless. In the *Zibaldone* Leopardi speaks of the limitless as of a non-thing, resolving the aporia with the proposal of a limit which is not external but internal to the thing itself: the "between," the world in-between, the "Zwischenwelt" that we find in the "bildnerisches Denken" of Klee, or in Rilke or Proust. The limit is not a frontier but a threshold: a place of transit, exchange, change and transfiguration. This is the perspective that Bataille lacks and it is this lack that dilutes the take of his erotology. It is not only the thing of habit that falls into the limitless, but also the gesture that transgresses it.

175. On apathy cf. *OC*, VII, p. 259 and passim.

176. *L'Érotisme*, *OC*, X, p. 13.

177. This citation and those in the following paragraph are located in *Frammenti postumi* 1882-1884, in *Opere*, eds. G. Colli and M. Montinari VII, I, 2 (Milano: Adelphi, 1986), 21[6], 15[43], 16[4], 17[1], 13[1], 22[3].

178. It is curious but interesting to observe how Benjamin too clashed with the same aporia in *Passagen-Werk*: the attempt to anchor a substantially a-dialectic thought to the Hegelian dialectic leads both Bataille and Benjamin to reach a deadlock before the necessity, implicit in their thought, of a theory of the symbol capable of comprehending the unresolvled and unresolvable coexistence of contradictions. This explains too Benjamin's "passion" for allegoresis, who states that allegory is a "salvation" compared to myth and symbol. This also explains Bataille's allegorical fury, as salvation with respect to the supreme transgression: that of thinking the different together. The purple labia of *Madame Edwards* thus signify *only* the necessity of total ostentation, the shit of Abbot C. signifies *only* the damnation of excrement and refuse. Each winds up not signifying enough, winds up forcing the plurality that these texts tried to grasp into a single meaning, a single gesture, which is a reduction to a unity: the classic gesture of habitual philosophy and thought.

179. The statement of S. Weil's in *Q*, III, p. 86 is the real turning-point, which Bataille reaches at the end without formulating it with equal clarity.

180. S. Weil, *Q*, II, pp. 14 and 44.

181. Dostoyevsky states: "Beauty is a terrible and frightening thing, because it is undefinable and one cannot define it, because God has given us nothing but enigmas. Here the two roads unite, here all contradictions coexist." With regard to this "beauty that will save the world" cf. F. Dostoevsky, *I fratelli Karamazov* and *L'idiota*, in *Romanzi e taccuini*, ed. E. Lo Gatto, trans. L. S. Boschian et al. (Firenze: Sansoni, 1958), vol. 5, p. 174, and vol. 2, p. 470. With regard to these themes I must refer again to *Asterischi*, in which an initial itinerary of the theme of beauty is mapped out through Baudelaire, Dostoyevsky, Proust, and Weil. Cf. as well my *Bellezza e verità* (Milano: Feltrinelli, 1990) and *L'enigma della bellezza* (Milano: Feltrinelli, 1991).

182. S. Weil, *Q*, III, pp. 95 and 119.

183. S. Weil, *Q*, III, p. 43.

184. These statements by Baudelaire, enigmatic outside of the context constructed here, are found in the personal observations of *Fusées*, in *Oeuvres complètes*, ed. C. Pichois (Paris: Gallimard, 1975), I.

185. "Kata physin" is the incipit of Aristotle's *Poetics*. The citations from Bataille are, again, with reference to *L'Érotisme*.

186. W. Benjamin, *Parigi capitale del XIX secolo*, p. 703.

Index

alterity, 6, 8, 16-17, 28, 32-33, 41, 45, 48, 66, 77, 109n, 115n; see also, mythologizing
Anti-Oedipus, 41
aorgic, 24
apathy, 46, 99-103, 120n
apparatus, 11, 17, 42, 45, 46, 57, 59-76, 115n
Aristotle, 105, 117n, 121n
Aron, J.-P., 105, 117n, 121n
Asor Rosa, A., 22, 77, 108n, 109n
atopy, 55, 82, 93, 103, 107n, 110n, 120n
autonomy, 15, 18, 22, 48, 76-77; myth of, 108n; see also, discourse
avant-garde, 39, 69

Baader-Meinhof, 47
Bataille, G., 1-2, 8-9, 81-106 *passim*, 116n-121n
Baudelaire, C., 84, 87, 95, 104, 105n, 118n, 121n
Baudrillard, J., 115n, 116n
beauty, 7, 79-106 *passim*, 120n, 121n; the look, 100-06; and thought, 7, 94; and ethics, 9
Benjamin, W., 3, 6, 25, 84, 105, 109n, 118n, 120n, 121n
Bleu du ciel, La, 93
Bodei, R., 3, 5, 7, 14, 24, 43, 107n, 108n, 109n, 112n, 115n
body, 17, 23, 43, 50, 52, 57, 59, 71, 104, 113n; social, 28, 47, 60; ideological, 36, 49, 65; signs, 44, 51; power, 68-69, 115n
border, 3, 6, 52, 82; and discourse, 77; see also, limen, threshold
Bréton, A., 34, 11n, 117n
Brothers Karamazov, The, 7

Cacciari, M., 3, 5, 6, 23, 108n, 109n, 111n, 115n, 116n
Calasso, 86
Chandos, Lord, 32
chaos, 45
classical, 32, 38, 45; see reason, classical
contradictions; and beauty, 7, 103-106; and reason, 15-16, 23-25, 28, 30, 48, 50-51, 74, 76; and discourse, 18-22, 66, 103, 120n; psychoanalysis, 34-40, 99, 121n
communication, 15, 24, 83, 89-94
Conrad, J., 66
consumption; truth of, 87, 94-96, 98, 106; see also expenditure, production
crisis; reason, 3-4, 5-6, 8, 14-19, 22-23, 29-48, 61, 65-66, 107n, 108n; norms, 29; psychoanalysis, 32-34, 40, 112n; economy, 74; see also discourse, Marxism
critical, 1-3, 16, 31, 35, 41, 60, 73, 78; reason, 8, 33, 46, 55

Dalmasso, 49
Daseinanalyse, 38
death (die), 32, 83, 85, 114n, 115n, 117n; subject, 8, 58; and Bataille, 83, 85-89, 90-91, 97-102, 105-106

de-creation, 93-94, 119n; and death 97-98
Deleuze, G., 1, 2, 8, 16, 17, 21, 24, 40, 41-47, 53-54, 71, 108n, 111n, 112n, 115n
De Maistre, J., 87-88, 118n
desire, 15, 16, 22, 27-30, 33-34, 40-43, 71, 97, 103, 105, 112n; without object, 16, 20, 98; and other, 28, 98; and economy, 44, 59; see also machines
dialect, 19, 29, 32, 34, 74
dialectic (late-dialectic, a-dialectic), 17, 28, 58, 59, 65, 70, 98, 102-05, 109n, 110n; unconscious, 41
discourse, 14, 32-35, 60-66, 69, 70-74, 76, 78, 112n; reason, 15-16, 21-22, 27; political, 18, 28, 45-48; crisis, 19-20, 99, 100; other, 21, 58, 77; Freud/Lacan, 37-41, 49-55, 76, 109n, 111n
disorder, 88, 97
disorientation, 43, 45, 53
Dostoyevsky, F., 7, 103, 121n
Durkheim, É., 89

Eco, U., 1
Economie libidinal, 44-47
economy, 16, 36, 43, 60, 62, 84, 82, 94-95; libidinal, 16-17, 44, 112n, 118n
Écrits, 38-49 passim
"effective" history, 57-59
ego, 33-35; see unconscious
eros, 9, 50, 82, 85, 92, 96, 100, 101, 103-04, 106; see logos
eroticism, 85, 98-101, 105
ethnology, French school of, 82, 89, 116n
evil, 87-88, 90, 92, 94-95
expenditure, 22, 60, 82, 88-89, 95, 118n
experience, 51, 53, 55, 63, 64, 91, 95, 96, 98, 99, 101, 106

Flaubert, G., 83, 88, 120n
Foucault, M., 1, 2, 5, 8, 11, 13, 16, 21, 24, 35, 57, 58-66, 70-78, 107n, 108n, 113n, 114n, 115n, 116n
fragmentary discourse, 77, 83-86, 90, 94
Freud, S., 3, 13, 19-21, 24, 29-39, 41-44, 47-49, 55, 59, 60, 63, 65, 74, 108n-112n, 114n, 115n, 118n

Gargani, A., 3, 5, 107n, 108n, 109n
gaze, 9, 73, 79, 81, 83-87, 104, 106
genealogy, 58, 63, 69, 71, 73, 74, 107n, 113n
Givone, S., 7
gnosis, gnostic, 91, 93, 119n, 120n
Goethe, J., 32, 110n
Guattari, F., 17, 21, 40-44, 47, 53-54, 71, 111n, 112n

Hegel, G., 14, 39, 72, 74, 76, 102, 107n, 116n, 120n
Heidegger, M., 19, 39, 83, 117n, 118n
heterotopia, 71, 73
Histoire de l'oeil, 85, 98, 101
History of Sexuality, The, 61
Hofmannsthal, 32
Hölderlin, 7, 24

id, 34; see unconscious
idealization, 9; negative, 19, 27, 29
ideology, 8, 20, 21, 28, 30, 34, 35, 36, 37, 42, 46, 58, 60; see also, body, discourse
Idiot, The, 7
il piccolo hans, 49, 113n
imperialism, 43
irrationalism; 36, 45, 108n, 115n; reason, 16-17;
Islam, 96

Index • 125

Jervis, G., 27, 109n
justice (injustice, unjust), 7, 62; see also Truth

Kafka, F., 3, 17, 25, 39, 83, 100, 108n, 111n, 118n, 120n
Kant, I., 8, 105, 111n
Kraus, 32
Kuhn, T., 19, 108n

Lacan, J., 1, 2, 5, 8, 20-21, 38-40, 44, 49, 50, 53, 54, 55, 73, 109n, 111n
Lacanianism (Lacanians), 8, 16, 17, 21, 38, 39, 40, 41, 48, 49, 53, 56, 76, 109n, 111n
Lakatos, I., 19, 108n
Left, the, 2, 3, 16, 28, 39, 41, 76, 115n
L'enigma della bellezza, 9
Levy, B.-H., 75, 115n
L'expérience intérieure, 84, 91
Lied von der Erde, 32
Lamaism, 96
language, 14, 21, 24, 40, 48, 64-68, 72-73, 76, 104, 113n; truth of, 17, 50; rational, 20, 29, 52-55, 77; strong, 22; mythology, 23; power, 67; game, 53
Larmes d'Eros, Les, 82, 96, 101
liberation, 15, 35, 42, 49, 69-72, 95, 119n
limen, 6, 104; see also border, threshold
literature, 37, 100, 102, 111n
L'histoire de l'erotisme, 98, 101
logos, 9, 50, 76, 100, 103, 106; see reason, Truth, eros
Lyotard, J.-F., 8, 16, 17, 40, 44, 45, 46, 47, 53, 112n, 115n

machines; 42, 50, 112n; see also molar, desiring
madness, 14, 29, 35, 44, 45, 62, 63, 64, 68, 72, 73, 74, 114n

Madness and Civilization, 73
Mahler, G., 32
Mallarmé, S., 39
Marx, K., 16, 19, 35, 46, 47, 64, 68, 74, 109n, 111n, 114, 115n
Marxism, 2, 16, 46, 64, 68, 69, 70, 74, 96, 107n, 108n; and Freud, 35-37, 43, 55; and power, 75
Mauss, 89, 91
Mephistopheles, 32
modernity, 5, 7, 88, 118n
molar, 42, 70, 71
Moro, A., 5
Musil, R., 3, 57
myth, mythology, 4. 6, 8, 17, 18, 19, 23, 27, 42, 43, 55, 66, 70, 76, 77, 107n, 108n, 120n

needs, 15-18, 20, 22, 23, 27, 36, 39, 41, 47, 55, 65, 71, 108n, 112n, 113n; genealogy of, 60-62; see also, theory
neo-classical reason, 16, 19, 21, 35, 37, 54, 61, 72; see reason, classical
neo-platonic, 91
Nietzsche, F., 3, 17, 19, 30, 34, 43, 58-66 passim, 74, 84, 92, 94, 99, 101, 102, 106, 108n, 111n-115n
"Nietzsche, Genealogy, History," 58-59
Notion de dépense, La, 82, 84

Other, 4, 7, 18, 21, 22, 24, 27, 28, 29, 37, 40, 44, 66, 75, 98, 106, 110n, 116n

"Painter of Modern Life, The," 95
pathos; 87, 100, 106, 117n, see apathy
Part maudite, La, 9, 84, 90, 99
philosophy, 3, 4, 5, 6, 7, 8, 20, 21, 34, 35, 37, 38, 46, 49, 50, 52, 61, 62, 65, 72, 75, 76, 82, 83,

87, 100, 102, 106; nouveaux, 75, 76; French, 1, 2, 81, 82
Plato, 6, 83, 104, 117n; see also neo-platonic
plurality (pluralism), 14, 16, 19, 20, 22, 24, 28, 30, 33, 34, 43, 45, 49, 53, 54, 66, 69, 73, 83, 109n, 110n, 120n
poetry, 22, 82, 91
potlatch, 89, 90, 95
power, 18, 30-31, 36, 43, 46, 47, 50, 58, 64-77, 103, 113n;
Foucault, 16, 59-61, 107n, 113n; rationality, 17, 19; norm, 29
production; knowledge, 52, 60; economic, 89, 94-95, 106; see also consumption
Proust, M., 81, 103, 105, 120n, 121n
psychoanalysis, 31, 32, 34, 37, 38, 40, 49, 110n, 112n; discourse, 20, 28
29, 38, 41; Marxism, 35, 69; see also Freud, Lacan

RAF, 47
rationality, 13-17, 20, 22, 24, 27, 31, 36-37, 48; see also discourse, irrationality
reason, 5, 8, 14, 15, 17, 19-23, 24, 27, 28, 31, 36, 39, 41, 49, 58, 64, 65, 73, 74, 76, 77, 84, 86, 100, 103, 107n, 109n, 117n; classical, 4, 8, 14, 17, 23, 32, 48, 54, 74; strong, 22; plurality, 49, 54; monistic, 16, 21, 45; machines, 42-43
real, 3, 6, 15, 27, 29, 39, 42, 43, 44, 45, 46, 48, 50, 55, 72, 85, 94, 97, 102, 103, 104; plurality, 14, 22, 23, 33, 46, 83
reality, 17, 20, 21, 22, 24, 25, 28, 29, 30, 34, 35, 36, 39, 41, 42, 45, 48, 52, 53, 54, 62, 72, 85, 89, 93, 95, 100; principle, 29

Red Brigade, 5
rhizome (rhizomatic), 42-43, 56, 111n, 112n
Right, the, 41, 115n
Rilke, R., 3, 45, 104, 106, 112n, 120n
Rivière, P., 64-68, 73-77, 114n, 115n
Rovatti, P., 3, 108n, 112n

sacrifice, 25, 87, 88, 90-97, 100, 106
semblance, 50-52, 113n
Seve, 36
science, 15, 19, 24, 39, 40, 46, 75, 88, 90, 95, 110n; 69-72, 75, 89, 94
silence, 21, 32, 39, 41, 48, 57, 63-68, 73-77, 114n
Silence and the Word, The, 3, 6
Smith, Patti, 43
Somme athéologique, La, 91
sovereignty, 99, 100, 116n
strong discourse, 16; reason, 21, 22
struggle, 31, 36, 47, 51, 54-55, 59, 66, 68-70, 78; political, 7, 15, 18, 19, 115n; knowledge, 24
subject, 6, 21-22, 29, 30, 36, 38, 40, 48, 51, 58, 66, 69, 77, 91, 106; weak, 6; death of, 8
subjectivity, 8, 18, 19, 100, 106
super-ego, 33-35, 55, 58; see unconscious
surrealism, 82, 111n, 116n, 117n

terrorism, 3, 5
theology, 6, 39
theory, 23, 36, 44, 53, 55, 91, 120n; French, 1; art, 7; logos, 9; needs, 16, 59, 108n, 113n; subject, 36; language, 55, 120n; power, 67, 69
therapy (therapeutic), 31, 34, 38, 87, 117n
threshold, 6, 7, 99, 104, 120n; see

limen, border
Tsvetayeva, M., 83
tragedy, 7, 32, 87
transversality, 43, 77, 111n
Truth, 7, 17, 19-21, 29-31, 34-35, 38-41, 44, 50-51, 53, 58-68, 76, 83, 84, 86, 95-97, 101, 104, 109n, 117n, 119n; true things, 24-25; see also, reason, justice, pluralism

unconscious, 23, 28-30, 33-34, 38, 41-42, 97, 109n, 110n, 112n; see also ego, super ego, id, utopia, 21, 34, 46, 71

Valery, P., 83, 117n

values (dis-values), 17-19, 22, 28-29, 41, 60, 69
Vattimo, G., 1, 6
Veca, S., 3, 23, 107n-109n, 111n, 112n
Verdiglione, A., 49-55, 109n, 112n, 113n

weak subject, 6, 73
Weber, M., 19, 36, 107n
Weil, S., 7, 9, 81, 90, 92, 93, 94, 97, 100, 103, 104, 119n-121n
Wittgenstein, L., 19, 23, 36, 48, 108n, 109n

Zarathustra, 44, 55, 112n
Zola, E., 88, 104